PEOPLE

A DAY WITH A CEO®

BRIAN MOORE

Copyright © 2012 by Brian Moore
All rights reserved.
ISBN: 0615665101
ISBN-13: 978-0615665108

WHY THIS BOOK?

This book has been created as a result of several decades of General Management experience covering many companies in different industries predominantly in the USA, Europe and Asia. The companies have been of varying size ranging from small family businesses through to publicly traded companies. Most of this experience has been gained as a group CEO directly leading a central team and over seeing the Profit and Loss performance of many subsidiary company teams running stand-alone businesses

The paradox is that as my career progressed and life became more complicated then the basic requirements of the General Management role appeared to be much simpler. The need to keep focused on basic questions and the need to keep asking **WHY ARE YOU DOING THAT?** Became more relevant. *A key task of the top Executives in any organization is to simplify complex subjects for the team to understand and run with.*

This is the third book in the *A Day With a CEO* series and focuses on **PEOPLE** as the successful *Inspiring, Leading and Motivating* of people is absolutely fundamental to the success of any organization. Many of the subjects covered in this book are often described as the *Soft Skills* of management, which I take exception to, as anyone who deals with people on a regular basis will tell you that this is one of the *Hardest* aspects of the job.

This is a planned follow on to the first two books — the first was a **HANDBOOK** for the General Manager and the second focused on **FINANCE**. This is the third book in a planned series of *A Day With a CEO* books that explain the role of a General Manager.

Although targeted at General Managers the content will be of use to anyone interested in how a business should be managed, especially early career managers with aspirations to become a General Manager. It will also be of use to provide to anyone that has the most important task which is to *manage and develop yourself!*

This is a book that I wish that I had at the start of my career to act as a **People Guide.** *I would certainly still be carrying it with me.*

INDEX

INTRODUCTION
People	6
You	7
Personal	8
Motivation v. Manipulation	9
Who Am I?	10-11
Flow Down Principle	12-13
Our Belief System	14-15

LIFE FORCE AND THE CIRCLE OF DEPENDENCE
(The concept of "Total Motivation")

Introduction	17-31
Circle of Dependence	32-46
People Skills	47-55
Energy	56
Emotions	57
Life Force Recap	58

RELATED SUBJECTS
Leadership v. Management	60-61
How To Be A Good Boss & Leader	62-63
Power & Politics	64
Under-rated Leadership Skills	65
Organizations Charts	67
The Law	68
People In High Places	69
Self-Help Books	70
Sales & Negotiation	71
Measuring Costs and Productivity	72-73
Managing the Boss	74
15 / 70 / 15 Principle	75
Dealing With Difficult People	77
Protecting People's Time	78-79

INDEX

CONCLUDING THOUGHTS
    Performance   82-83
    Difficult Decisions   84
    Power of Belief   85
    Looking After YOU   86
    Big Secret   87
    Pet Theory   88

APPENDICES
    Stories   90-101
    Check Lists   102-106
    Common Terms and Abbreviations   107-108

PEOPLE

Many managers have said to me that the hardest part of the job is managing people.

My response: **GIVE UP!**

That is the first mistake. The job is to INSPIRE, LEAD and MOTIVATE.

Manage yourself and encourage everyone else to manage themselves.

The better the job they do of that, the greater the requirement is to

INSPIRE, LEAD & MOTIVATE.

Good PEOPLE cannot be "Managed."

THE REQUIREMENT

All organizations require to have good people that are highly motivated and effective.

THE COST

People are usually one of the highest costs of any organizations.

THE MANAGERIAL OBJECTIVE

Maximum EFFECTIVENESS of the PEOPLE at optimum cost.

TERMINOLOGY

This book is using the terms
PEOPLE
WHO ARE
PAID TO WORK

The various terms used to describe PEOPLE in the workplace have been avoided. People are concerned much more about how they are treated, respected and made to feel than what they are called. Of course there is nothing wrong with using what you consider to be a more positive label, if it works. Just remember under every label is a person that needs to be respected and treated appropriately.

The book title **PEOPLE** is deliberate. No other words really apply, maybe "Understanding," but that I considered to be a touch arrogant. But certainly not "Managing People." See the top point! The book is about personal experiences and opinions.

> **This starts and finishes with YOU!**

YOU !

This book is about you and your personal development. It is intended to make you think about the role of General Management in a BUSINESS organization and how it applies to you and your performance.

The book is full of opinions and experiences; some will work for you, some will not. Some will work some of the time, some will not. This is the nature of life and dealing with people in particular.

Leading a business organization is largely an interpersonal process, so any skills that you can develop to become better at dealing with relationships and developing your skill set to influence and inspire other people the better.

Take from this book what you want to make you a more effective manager and leader.

You are ultimately responsible for your own personal development, make a good job of it!

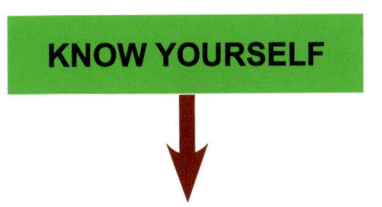

KNOW YOURSELF

↓

Leadership Style / Learning Style / Myers Briggs / Best Time of Day / Strengths and Weaknesses / Psychometric Tests / Negotiating Style

PERSONAL

LACK OF PERSONAL ACCOUNTABILITY: A KEY REASON BUSINESSES FAIL

WHAT WE HEAR

WE WORK TO LIVE, NOT LIVE TO WORK
IT'S JUST A JOB
GET A LIFE
KEEP WORK SEPARATE
STAY DETACHED
IT'S NOT PERSONAL, IT'S BUSINESS

This is fine for the vast majority of the working population

**In my view, however if you are the top Exec / GM of a business, it is
A TOTALLY PERSONAL EXPERIENCE**

How you do your job could affect the personal experiences of thousands of people. Not only your team members, but also their loved ones, dependents, etc.

This is an overwhelming sense of personal responsibility that I would wake up with every day.

I can guarantee with almost 100% certainty that when you are talking to anyone on your team about anything important, especially change, just one thought is going through their heads.

How does this affect me personally?

MOTIVATION v. MANIPULATION

IMPORTANT
WE REQUIRE TO DEAL WITH THIS RIGHT UP FRONT!

*This is very important because **MOTIVATION** is a great people skill. **MANIPULATION** is a destructive force. The reason it is important is because the **ACTION COMPONENT** is often the **SAME**. The difference is our personal intent and our motivation in launching the initial action.*

EXAMPLE

You employ an intern and then have them doing mundane work week after week. The positive MOTIVATOR is to provide that intern with a feeling for the work experience and to illustrate to them what so many mundane jobs are all about. The MANIPULATIVE action is to just use the intern on an indefinite basis as cheap labor to avoid hiring a permanent person.

BE CAREFUL

People are much smarter than you may think and they can usually tell if and when they are being manipulated. Guess what? If they have any doubts, which way will they go? Do they usually give management the benefit of the doubt?

WHO AM I?

Who would I like to be? Engaged? Effective? Inspirational?

The most important job we all face is to manage ourselves, the better job we do of it the more effective and valuable we are. I am sure that most of you will have heard the expression "The only constant is change." Actually:

The only real constant in your life is you.

Please use the ideas in this book to ensure that you are well prepared for what life deals to you.

"Who I would like to be?"

This book provides a lot of personal experience resulting from dealing with many people in the business world at many different levels. Take from it what you want to improve your PEOPLE SKILLS and to help towards becoming the type of person / leader / manager that you would like to be.

FINDING OUT ABOUT YOU

The most important project that you have is to manage your own personal development. In order to do this effectively then you need to be constantly evaluating your own performance and developing training programs and strategies to improve. The more senior the position that you have in a business, then the more important it is to manage your own development. When in a junior position you will probably be constantly reviewed and sent on training courses. As you progress up the corporate ladder this becomes more of a self-motivating process. In order to review progress you need to find out about yourself.

WAYS TO FIND OUT ABOUT YOU

- Ask people who you respect and trust. Avoid fishing for compliments.
- Formal company reviews. Above and below. 360-degree exercises.
- Psychometric tests. Many examples like Myers Briggs. Note that you will change, so it is a good idea to keep reviewing these results.
- Evaluation products that give you an insight into specific areas. For example, Learning style, Negotiating style, Energy level.
- Observe your own behavior to see how you perform in certain situations or at certain times of the day.
- Look for evidence of the results of your behavior in the actions of others.
- Recognize your own strengths and weaknesses and build a team that supports or compensates for them.
- Seek mentoring advice / help that is independent and not involved in your day-to-day dramas.

HOW TO IMPROVE

Monitor and improve performance.
Seek out training programs.
Seek advice from more experienced executives.
Try different things and experiment. Learn from mistakes.

PASS YOUR EXPERIENCE ON AND HELP OTHERS TO IMPROVE

THE FLOW DOWN PRINCIPLE

The PYRAMID is a representation of the key tasks of a General Manager and you will see that "INSPIRE and LEAD" is one of the three most important tasks of the GM. This of course applies to INSPIRING and LEADING PEOPLE. It starts at the top of an organization and flows down. The top man or woman sets the tone.

TONE FROM THE TOP?

Trees die from the top.
~Peter Drucker

BUSINESS BASICS   PYRAMID OF SUCCESS

TOP 3 OBJECTIVES
- Make money
- Inspire and lead
- Do RIGHT things

MAKE MONEY

INSPIRE AND LEAD	DO *RIGHT* THINGS
PEOPLE	CUSTOMERS	FINANCE
OPERATIONS	INNOVATE	NEGOTIATON	MEASURE

GETTING THINGS DONE

STRATEGIC PLAN / MISSION

Make sure things GET DONE

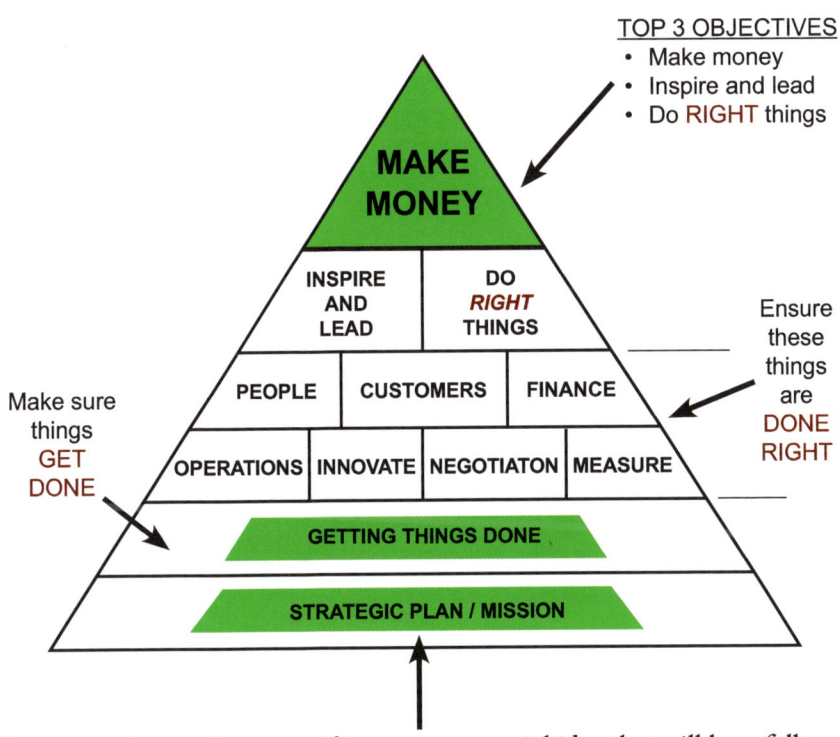

Ensure these things are DONE RIGHT

All businesses have to have a guiding entrepreneurial idea that will hopefully make it money. This idea can be expressed in a few different formats.

Mission Statement / Strategic Intent / Business Plan

The success of any business will ultimately depend on if this idea is able to create wealth.

The number one objective of the GM is to understand and believe in this idea and its capability to make money.

The GM will be required to understand and "SIGN IN" to the main strategic intent of the business.

Keep this model in your head at all times.

OUR BELIEF SYSTEMS

COMMON SENSE IS COMMON

You think so many things are obvious to everyone because they are obvious to you? Never take anything for granted. If it is important, ask the obvious questions.

TELEPATHY EXISTS

I have had this conversation many times. Someone starts to tell me about what some one else has or has not done. My usual question is "Have you told them?" and the usual reply. "Well no, they should have known that." We tend to assume a lot.

STRANGERS ARE WONDERFUL

Some managers have a tendency to hire and fire. Behind these actions is an implicit believe that there is someone out there that we have never met, know nothing about, yet somehow will come in and be effective in our business. This may be true but the odds are about 50% of that being true. Before sending for a stranger make sure that all options have been explored to get what you want from the person in the job already.

PLANS WORK

Planning is a major time activity of management. We plan formally and informally long-term, short-term, mid-term, etc. Just be aware that the planning process may well be a good learning experience be prepared for the plans to not work out as expected.

OUR BELIEF SYSTEMS

TIME IS INFINITE

We are nearly always on the run and running out of time. We plan incrementally and rarely look at the whole conflicts that the various plans interacting with each other produce. These plans typically indicate an assumption on our part that we have plenty of time. One further thing, "Time Management" is not a real activity. Time can never be managed, it is us that requires the management.

PEOPLE LISTEN

We usually communicate in transmit mode and value the success of the communication by the quality of the delivery. An exercise that would test your communication ability. For a week or so whenever you have a communication event, a meeting or telephone call, whatever, when you believe that you have finished ask a couple of questions. What have I just told you? What are you now going to do? The answers are usually interesting, depressing and sometimes scary.

I RAN THIS WELL, SO I CAN RUN THAT WELL

In the POP record industry the "ONE HIT WONDER" concept is well understood. The same happens in business except that the price of finding out can be very high.

IT IS ALL ABOUT ME

We are nearly all motivated by self-interest. It is a very dependable behavior characteristic. Be aware as it can be useful, but also dangerous and unfortunately depressing.

PEOPLE & PERFORMANCE

THE
LIFE FORCE
(And "THE CIRCLE OF DEPENDENCY")

THAT GETS THINGS DONE

The next few pages are based upon the theory that we have a larger **"LIFE FORCE"** within us, but certain factors that we deal with on a "Day-By-Day" basis will impact how we perform.

This is a concept of
"TOTAL MOTIVATION."

LIFE FORCE & CIRCLE OF DEPENDENCY
IN THE WORKPLACE

We all have an inner LIFE FORCE that defines us. The way we are! The way we are viewed! The way we think! Our value systems! And ultimately, the way we behave! (Our motivational persona, as it were.)

This LIFE FORCE is a constantly changing part of us and it is effected by 5 KEY AREAS that surround us.

Our environment at the workplace. The basic things that we have like pay, secure workplace, nice surroundings, tools to do the job, etc. WE could call this "GENERIC MOTIVATION."

How fit and strong are we? Do we have the basic ENERGY to do the job?

Do we have the PEOPLE SKILLS to be able to communicate and operate in a group of people, or maybe talk to customers?

How are EMOTIONS — are we able to easily deal with the world around us? Or are we constantly having to deal with our emotional reactions to what we are experiencing?

Do we have specific goals and targets? Are we skilled and trained enough to do them? Are we SPECIFICALLY MOTIVATED?

These 5 KEY AREAS are all important in their own right, but they all INTERACT with each other and affect our LIFE FORCE.

WHAT IS THE LIFE FORCE?

This could be defined as the way we behave and what makes us all unique individuals. It will be different for everyone with respect to its nature and strength. It is what defines us, it is how we drive ourselves. It is the mechanism that we use to manage how the 5 KEY AREAS affect us, or not? It is how people view us. It is the inner us. Many people will only see how we behave through the 5 KEY areas. Maybe never see past those areas into the real you.

LIFE FORCE

THE LIFE FORCE IN ACTION

The essential role of the life force is to look at what is happening in the CIRCLE OF DEPENDENCY and the 5 KEY AREAS. It is then constantly checking and moving between these boxes to ensure that BALANCE is maintained and that we are able to perform effectively.

We use our LIFE FORCE to obtain strength from the strong areas in order to deal with any issues in the weak areas. It is important that the CIRCLE OF DEPENDENCE is not breached and our life force is not overrun. You will know if the life force is under attack because thoughts will develop in your head like:

I CAN DEAL WITH THIS?
THIS IS NOT GOING TO GET TO ME.

5 KEY AREAS
DEFINITIONS

AS RELATED TO THE WORKPLACE

GENERIC MOTIVATION
WORKPLACE SAFETY
ENVIRONMENT SUITABLE TO WORK IN
BASIC EMPLOYMENT CONDITIONS ARE ACCEPTABLE
WE WANT TO GO TO WORK
PAY AND BENEFITS ACCEPTABLE

EMOTIONS
HOW WE FEEL
HOW WE REACT TO SITUATIONS
DO WE FEEL SECURE

ENERGY
LEVEL OF PHYSICAL FITNESS
INTELLIGENCE / SKILL SET
POSITIVE ATTITUDE TO WORKING

PEOPLE SKILLS
ABILITY TO RELATE TO OTHER PEOPLE
COMMUNICATION SKILLS
FEEL INCLUDED AND ACCEPTED

SPECIFIC MOTIVATION
WELL-DEFINED GOALS
WE KNOW WHAT IS EXPECTED OF US
WE ARE TRAINED TO DELIVER WHAT IS EXPECTED

CIRCLE OF DEPENDENCY

Consider these 5 KEY AREAS as being in a circle to provide protection and to influence our LIFE FORCE at the center. The LIFE FORCE will also influence and control what is going on in the 5 KEY AREAS.

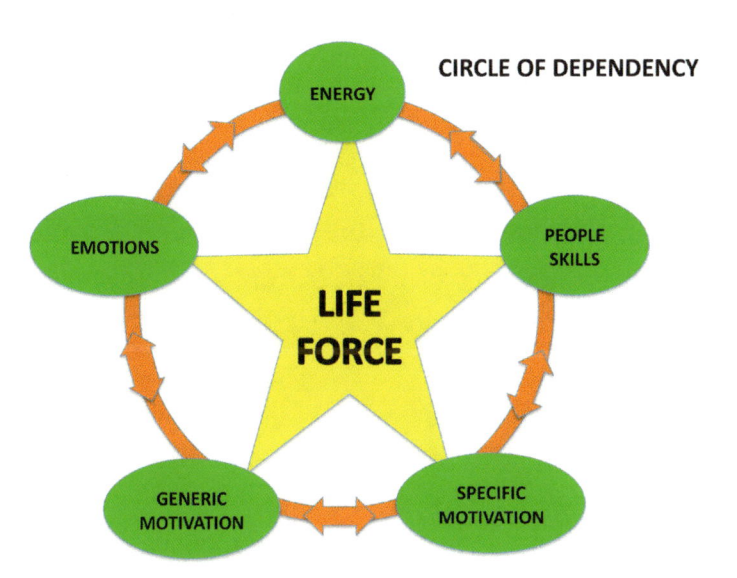

CIRCLE OF DEPENDENCY

- ENERGY
- PEOPLE SKILLS
- SPECIFIC MOTIVATION
- GENERIC MOTIVATION
- EMOTIONS

LIFE FORCE

A WAY TO LOOK AT A PERSON

We all have a CIRCLE OF DEPENDENCY and the stronger that it is, the more it enriches and develops our LIFE FORCE. The weaker the CIRCLE OF DEPENDENCY, the more involved that our LIFE FORCE has to become to get things done and function. We operate against the odds, as it were. If all else fails we just keep going driven by our LIFE FORCE!

Your responsibility is to develop your own CIRCLE OF DEPENDENCY and to behave in a way that we support and develop the CIRCLE OF DEPENDENCY of everyone that we come into contact with.

The next few pages will discuss these **5 KEY AREAS** and the **LIFE FORCE** and how they all relate to each other.

FACTORS THAT EFFECT THE 5 KEY AREAS

The 5 KEY AREAS are constantly changing and our LIFE FORCE is impacted by these changes and has to deal with these changes. This **EXPERIENCE** affects two fundamental areas.

HOW WE FEEL.

HOW WE ARE SEEN BY OTHERS. (ATTITUDE?)

BOTH OF THESE CAN SIGNIFICANTLY EFFECT OUR WORK PERFORMANCE

FACTORS THAT AFFECT THE 5 KEY AREAS

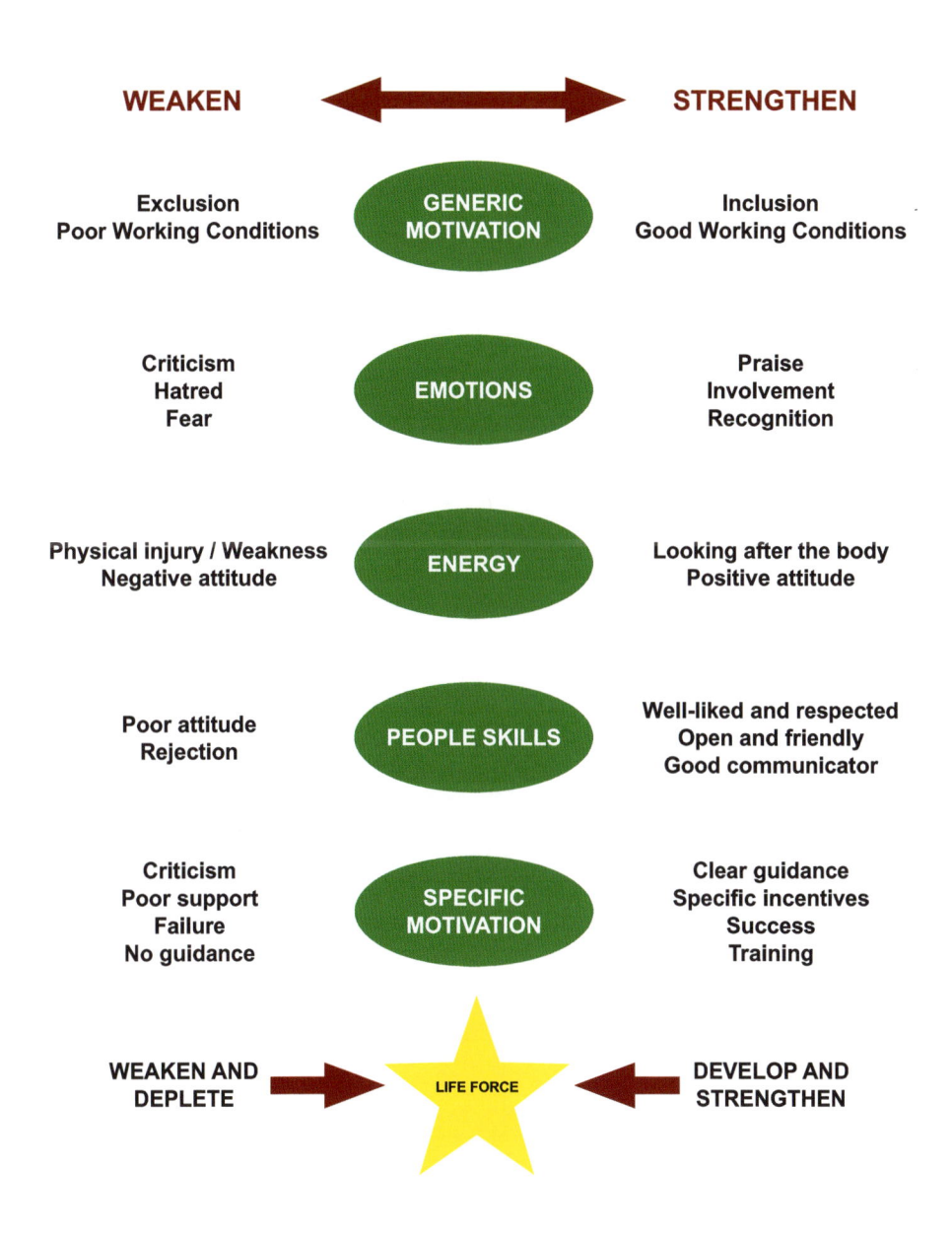

WEAKEN ⟷ **STRENGTHEN**

WEAKEN		STRENGTHEN
Exclusion Poor Working Conditions	**GENERIC MOTIVATION**	Inclusion Good Working Conditions
Criticism Hatred Fear	**EMOTIONS**	Praise Involvement Recognition
Physical injury / Weakness Negative attitude	**ENERGY**	Looking after the body Positive attitude
Poor attitude Rejection	**PEOPLE SKILLS**	Well-liked and respected Open and friendly Good communicator
Criticism Poor support Failure No guidance	**SPECIFIC MOTIVATION**	Clear guidance Specific incentives Success Training

WEAKEN AND DEPLETE → **LIFE FORCE** ← **DEVELOP AND STRENGTHEN**

THE 5 KEY AREAS
HOW WE FEEL!

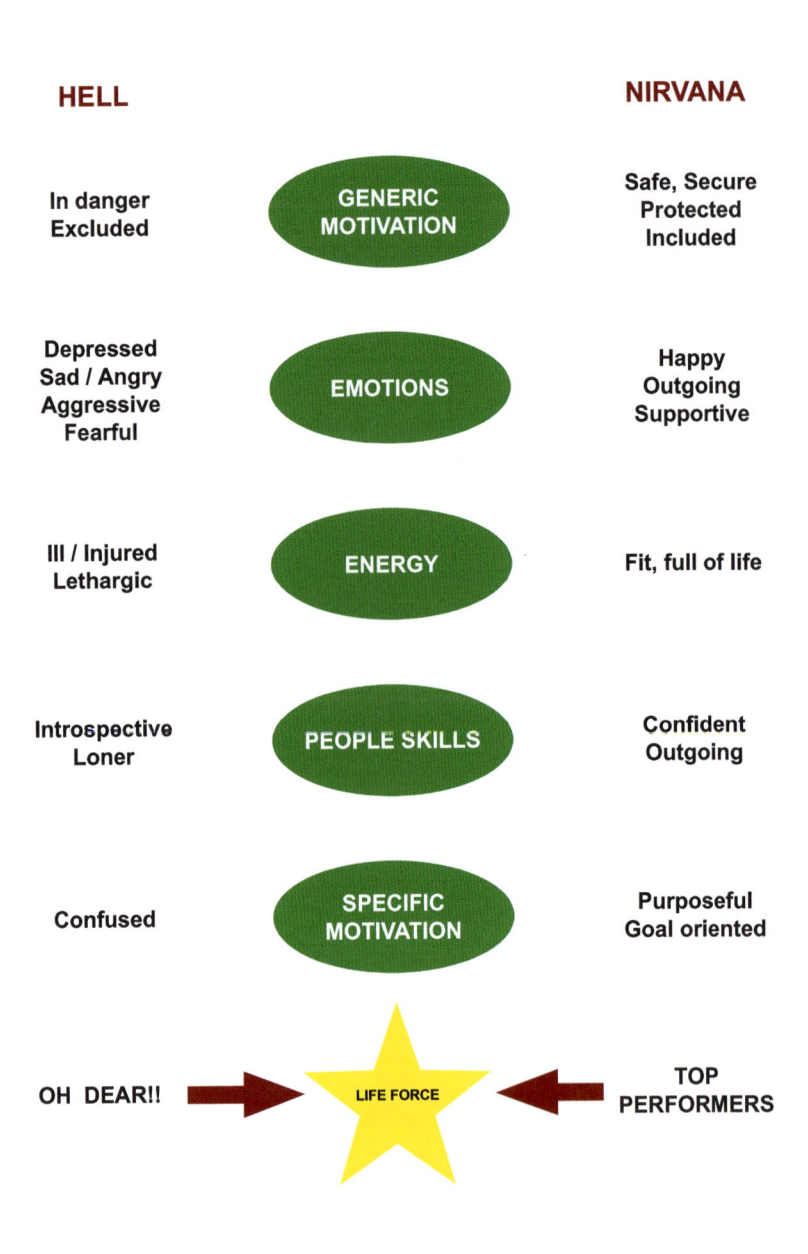

HELL   **NIRVANA**

HELL		NIRVANA
In danger / Excluded	**GENERIC MOTIVATION**	Safe, Secure / Protected / Included
Depressed / Sad / Angry / Aggressive / Fearful	**EMOTIONS**	Happy / Outgoing / Supportive
Ill / Injured / Lethargic	**ENERGY**	Fit, full of life
Introspective / Loner	**PEOPLE SKILLS**	Confident / Outgoing
Confused	**SPECIFIC MOTIVATION**	Purposeful / Goal oriented
OH DEAR!! →	**LIFE FORCE**	← TOP PERFORMERS

THE 5 KEY AREAS
HOW WE ARE SEEN OUR ATTITUDE!

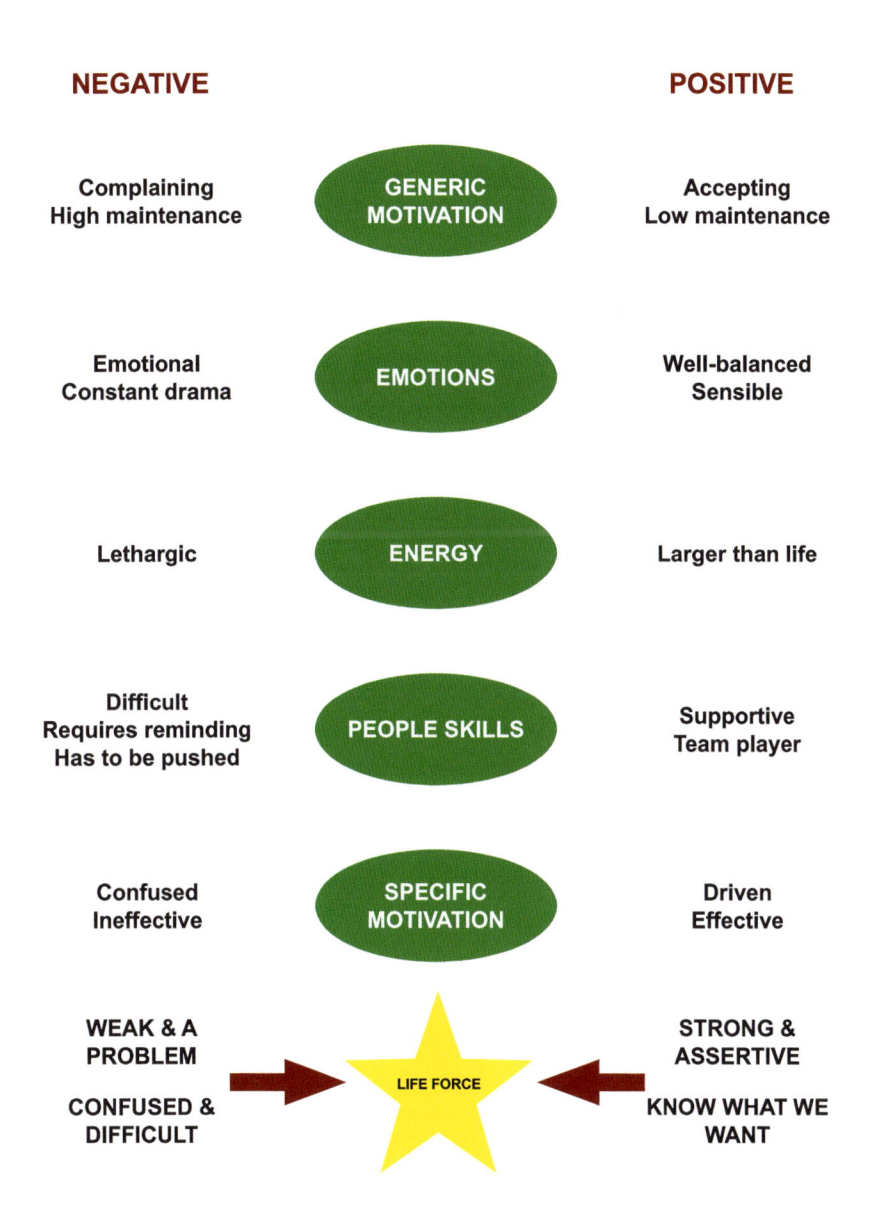

NEGATIVE		POSITIVE
Complaining High maintenance	**GENERIC MOTIVATION**	Accepting Low maintenance
Emotional Constant drama	**EMOTIONS**	Well-balanced Sensible
Lethargic	**ENERGY**	Larger than life
Difficult Requires reminding Has to be pushed	**PEOPLE SKILLS**	Supportive Team player
Confused Ineffective	**SPECIFIC MOTIVATION**	Driven Effective
WEAK & A PROBLEM CONFUSED & DIFFICULT	**LIFE FORCE**	STRONG & ASSERTIVE KNOW WHAT WE WANT

THESE ARE THE LABELS THAT PEOPLE JUDGE US BY. RIGHTLY OR WRONGLY.

DEVELOPING AND PROTECTING THE LIFE FORCE

The stronger the life force, then there is less for it to do to protect us from problems in the 5 KEY AREAS. If our circle is continually attacked at many levels our life force could become depleted, or indeed may become strengthened (character building adversity?). But the way we develop the life force is to look at the areas that may be particularly strong and then deploy them against any areas of weakness or where we may have a problem.

ABOVE ALL ELSE,
DO NOT LET THINGS DEPLETE THE LIFE FORCE
BECAUSE
THE LIFE FORCE IS
YOU!
IT IMPACTS HOW WE FEEL AND HOW WE ARE JUDGED.

A fairly common example of a depleted life force is unfortunately the person so debilitated by stress that they are unable to perform and have to leave the workplace. Management have a HUGE responsibility to protect themselves from this. They have an even bigger responsibility to ensure that they do not cause it in others. Unfortunately I see examples of bad management depleting peoples life force on regular basis. In many instances without realizing that they are doing it.

DEVELOPING AND PROTECTING THE LIFE FORCE

SOME EXAMPLES TO ILLUSTRATE HOW WE COMPENSATE

We are constantly having different experiences in the 5 KEY AREAS. We use our LIFE FORCE to move between these areas in order to create a good feeling and to negate any areas that may be not going so well.

EXAMPLES

The boss upsets you so go and have a workout

You have an emotional upset, so you use your people skills to talk it out.

You lose a valuable possession, so you use your emotional strength to put it in perspective.

MANY THOUSANDS OF OTHER WAYS. WHAT WORKS FOR YOU?

MANY MORE. THINK OF A FEW?

For most of us, most of the time this is an ongoing part of life and we get on with it and survive. Suffering the slings and arrows of fortune as it were. For some people, some of the time the 5 KEY AREAS may be under such attack, maybe all of them from different aspects that the **CIRCLE BECOMES OVERWHELMED** and our **LIFE FORCE IS THREATENED**. This is when we start to fell depressed, want to give up, quit, take time off, etc. This can be very serious in us and other people. We should be constantly checking to look after ourselves and each other. This is what being a responsible member of the human race is all about in my view.

EXAMPLES OF HOW PEOPLE INTERACTIONS IMPACT LIFE FORCE

How we react to the **EXPERIENCES** that we have in our 5 KEY AREAS will effect how we behave and how we relate to each other. Our behavior will therefore impact the 5 KEY AREAS of other people for better or worse. We should aim to make this interaction as positive as possible.

SOME POSITIVE EXAMPLES

We feel on top of the world and pass compliments on to other people.

We are blessed with wealth, so we pass some of it on to others.

Someone may be having difficulty doing something. We offer help and guidance.

We support the leader, and let it be known.

Proactive and inspirational.

SOME NEGATIVE EXAMPLES

Constant criticism of others.

Moaning about poor me. (Who really cares?)

Cynical comments about everything.

Nothing is ever good enough. In a bad way?

Little GENERIC MOTIVATION issues get us down. Coffee machine broken. World ending.

I am SURE that you can think of many more. Just giving you an idea.

NOTE FOR LEADERS

You should be injecting as much positive behavior into the team as possible and making sure that the team members look after each other in a positive way. Seek and destroy negative influences wherever possible.

What positive actions have you done to enhance someone's LIFE FORCE?

LIFE FORCE

THE BOTTOM LINE
(As this is a business book)

LIFE FORCE

Our **LIFE FORCE** drives how we behave and it is developed, depleted, strengthened, weakened by events in the workplace depending what is happening in the **5 KEY AREAS.** It is a collective and ongoing process related to what we **EXPERIENCE.** When all is going well in the 5 Areas our life force will grow. If things are going moderately badly, maybe a few issues, then our LIFE FORCE will also grow and deal with them. If the issues become too much, then our LIFE FORCE maybe will be over run and start to diminish.

A leader has a responsibility to make sure that the team has as many **POSITIVE EXPERIENCES** in the **5 KEY AREAS** as possible. This will result in a **HIGHLY MOTIVATED TEAM that "GET THINGS DONE."**

THE OUTSIDE WORLD

Of course all these experiences in the 5 KEY AREAS also apply to what is happening in the outside world. The world of work is impacted as we do not have two LIFE FORCES. As far as possible we may try to compartmentalize these two world in our LIFE FORCE, but a degree of crossover is inevitable. It is a question of degree. What happens at work could dramatically impact how our LIFE FORCE deals with our outside world. What is happening in our outside world could impact how our life force deals with the world of work. Be aware, only so much can be left at the door when we start WORKING!!

INTERACTION WITH OTHER PEOPLE

THE ACTIONS OF OTHER PEOPLE IMPACT OUR LIFE FORCE AND OUR ACTIONS IMPACT OTHER PEOPLE'S LIFE FORCES

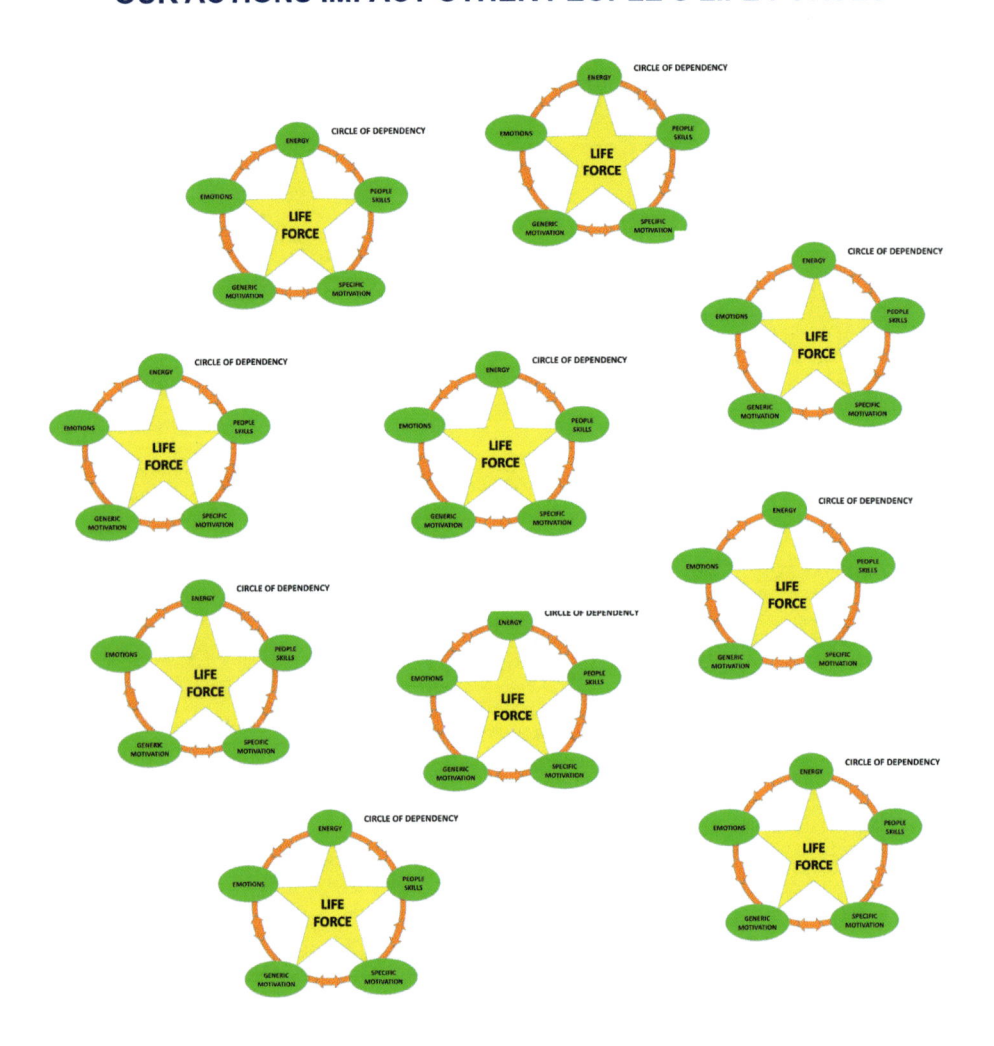

10 PEOPLE ALL RELATING TO EACH OTHER

NO COMBINATION OF ANY TWO PAIRINGS EACH ONE OF WHICH COULD BE AN ISSUE

30000 PLUS POTENTIAL COMBINATIONS

MAYBE THAT IS WHY DEALING WITH PEOPLE CAN BE DIFFICULT

GOING FOR GREEN (A QUICK AUDIT)

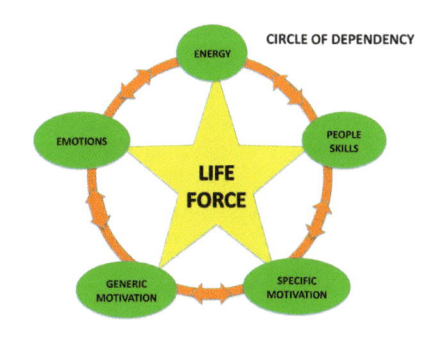

GREAT! EVERYTHING GOING WELL.

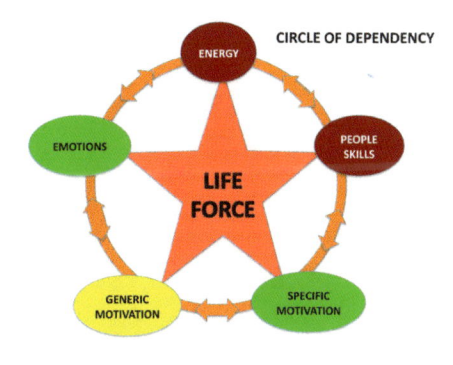

WORK IN PROGRESS.

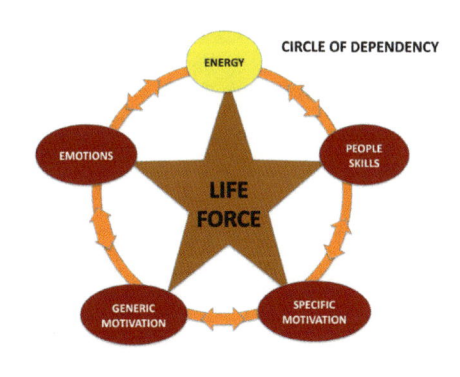

OH DEAR, YOU NEED A SERIOUS CHAT WITH YOURSELF OR SOMEONE?

UNHAPPY   NOT HAPPY   HAPPY

THE 5 KEY AREAS

These are discussed in more detail in the next few pages.

GENERIC MOTIVATION   **SPECIFIC MOTIVATION**

Motivation is a huge and fundamentally important subject because managers need it to get things done and *"People get things done."* Consequently they have to be motivated to do them. In this section are the basic building blocks from some of the classic founding fathers of motivation theory. In all your dealings with people remember a few basic points.

**You will not please all of the people all of the time.
People largely learn through personal experience, which can be slow.
People know about these things and you will not fool them.
People often focus on self-interest.**

Generic Motivation is largely an aspect of "Culture and Environment" in that you should create a mindset in your team that is positive and open to new ideas and willing to be motivated. People should ideally be enthusiastic and feel included. This is an important part of company culture. The creation of a "Generic Motivation" mindset in the team is a long haul and requires constant attention and work. Some of the major benefits of creating a successful Culture of GENERIC MOTIVATION will often be outside your immediate awareness. People will get on with things without too much direction and typically do the right thing. The objective is to make people feel positive about coming to work. What they do when they get there is more to do with Specific Motivation.

Specific or Task Motivation is much clearer to understand and often easy to do. If you require someone to do a specific task, you require to decide if they need educating or motivating, or both? For example, you could offer me a trillion dollars to play the violin, but it would not be possible as I have not been "Educated or Trained" to do it. (Mind you I may want to learn pretty damn quick!) On the other hand, you may want someone to work over the weekend and they clearly know what to do, so what will it take to motivate them to do it? It may be as simple as paying overtime rates or as complex as making many other different arrangements in order for them to agree.

The relationship between Generic Motivation and Specific Motivation is also important because if you do a good job creating a culture of positive Generic Motivation then the achievement of specific tasks within that culture becomes easier and it will often cost less. A switched-on, well-motivated team requires less financial incentive to carry out special tasks. A demotivated team in a toxic culture will be difficult to motivate. Disengaged people can be expensive in so many ways: sickness, efficiency, people turnover, constant training.

The next important point relates to a special word — "Feelings." How we feel about things drives so much of how we behave. Feelings are emotional responses to the many things that are happening to us in all aspects of our life, in and out of the workplace. This is a really hard area to understand and get right. We are all different and so many things can affect our feelings. No manager will never be able to get it right all of the time. Sometimes we have to just leave people alone to work things out for themselves. Always have in mind the following saying by Maya Angelo:

"I've learned that people will forget what you said, people will forget what you did, but people will never forget how you made them feel."

Be aware at all times that many of your actions will create an emotional response, so make sure that it is a positive one.

VOLTAIRE (1694-1778)

I include Voltaire the French philosopher not so much as a motivational guru, but it makes the point that learning takes so long as we usually have to experience things for ourselves to really learn. (How often do you touch a plate in a restaurant that you are told is hot?) Some of his comments and quotes are still so topical like "Common sense is far from common."

HAWTHORNE WORKS (1924-1932)

Chicago 1930, a Western Electric assembly plant (Hawthorne) with hundreds of workers using hand skills to assemble products was the subject of a study by Henry Landsberger. This was the early days of work-study when the scientific study of the workplace was in its infancy. Henry decided to set up a small team of assembly workers in a special room and try out various methods of assembly. The goal being to design the most efficient way of working within this group, which could subsequently be used by the whole workforce. For a few weeks he kept trying different techniques and after each change the performance improved, and inevitably the day came when he thought "this is it the perfect assembly method." Being a good scientist he wanted to test his theories, so he asked this special group to do some changes, which he had calculated would result in the performance going down.

Guess what, the performance actually went up, against the calculated logic.

This is called the "Hawthorne Effect" (well it was when I was a lad!). The point being that if you treat people in a special way, they will behave and react in a special way and often perform above and beyond logical expectations.
So much of what is considered modern day manufacturing processes like " Lean" are based around the inclusion of the person in the workplace. Success on these programs is in my view largely because you create this "Hawthorne Effect" on a systematic basis. The constant "inclusion" (a key word) of people is a key motivational factor.

Everyone usually likes to feel "Included."

HERZBERG (1968 book sold 1.2 million copies by 1987)

Another big favorite and he identified two specific concepts. The *"Middle State"* and the difference between "Hygiene factors" and "True motivators." I particularly like the concept of the middle state. For example, if you are not happy it does not always follow that you are unhappy. The middle state would be "Just not happy." The importance of this in motivational behavior is that I believe people will tolerate "Not being happy" for quite a long time. We can see examples of people just not being happy all around us. I even think that for many people this is their normal state of existence. However people will not usually tolerate "Being unhappy" on a long-term basis, they will want to do something about it. It is very hard to make people happy all the time, but it is not quite so hard as stopping them from being "Unhappy all the time."

The other area that is linked to this middle state is the way Herzberg categorized some of the more common motivational factors into "Hygiene Factors" and "True Motivators." The Hygiene Factors will stop us from being unhappy, but will not necessarily make us happy. The True Motivators will make us feel more included and consequently may make us happy. An example of these motivators:

HYGIENE FACTORS

Company policy
Pay & Benefits
Work conditions
Status
Personal life
Relationship with coworkers

If these things are right, they will not always make us happy.
If they are not right, we become very unhappy.

TRUE MOTIVATORS

Achievement
Recognition / Inclusion
Responsibility
Advancement
Growth

These are the positive motivators that will make us happy and perform better.

DALE CARNEGIE (1888 – 1955)

I am sure everyone must have read the book *"How to Win Friends and Influence People."* If not, do so immediately. Some really good stuff in this book like: Your favorite sound — your own name. Your favorite subject — you. Good as this may be and it does all work really well, I want to discuss the secondary effects. Read the book for headline points.

One of the problems of a well-known significant work is that it may become stale, as everyone knows it. For example, the sales person that starts down the line of questions about you, family, college, etc. can sometimes be irritating. It may even act as deterrent for you. The use of what you may consider to be obvious tactics. Do not be put off!

These tactics always work and you should override any instinct not to use them just because you may perceive them to be obvious. The reason is what I would term the secondary effect. When someone recognizes that you are using these well-known tactics to win their favor, they may well have an initial feeling of irritation. This is then often replaced with the secondary feeling that goes like this, "This person must view me as important that they are prepared to use this approach to win my favors." A secondary compliment by using the techniques.

Our most favorite sound — "Our Name"
Our most favorite subject — "Us"

MACHIAVELLI (1469 – 1527)

A warring prince in Italy that used to go round conquering and taking over villages to create a larger empire. A lot of that in those days! His views on how to deal with his conquered subjects and some of his views on motivation are outlined in a book called "The Prince," which is well worth a read, but can be heavy going. The expression "Very Machiavellian" applied to someone who has just done something underhand or devious. I did not get that from the book and with so many things in life, if you ask someone that uses that expression if they have read "The Prince" guess what, the answer usually is — "No!"

Machiavelli in my view has made two large contributions. "Bad news all at once." "Good news over time." Let me explain.

If for example, you are required to do a downsizing and have to let people go, but are not sure if it is maybe 50 or 60 people, then you announce on DAY 1 quickly what you think is the worst-case scenario. In this case, 60 people. If a week later you go back and reduce it to 50, that's good news. If on the other hand, you initially announce 50 then a week later another two, then a week later two more, etc., this creates a feeling long-term uncertainty and insecurity in the team.

For good news, deploy it over time to obtain the maximum effect. The salesperson that you would like to increase pay, give a large bonus and maybe provide a company car. If you do all this on DAY 1, the person will get used to the new situation pretty quickly after the initial euphoria. Then you have to deal with someone with higher aspirations. A better way to deal with this is to sit and discuss the situation with the person and agree over maybe a year (or two) certain targets, which if achieved, will be matched with these awards. You will probably have locked that person into the team for a couple of years in a positive way that everyone is happy with.

MASLOW (1943 Paper)

The *"Hierarchy of Needs"* is a major analytical tool developed by Maslow. Its levels can be used to determine where everyone on your team is at any particular time. They will change.

SELF-ACTUALIZATION

ESTEEM

LOVE / BELONGING

SAFETY

PHYSIOLOGICAL

Let me develop my views as to what these various levels mean in the work environment.

At the lowest levels most of us, most of the time feel that we have the basic physiological requirements to do the job and that we feel safe. Not always of course, and if this is not the case, then these areas require immediate attention unless it is an inherent part of the job, some jobs are just dangerous. The important thing about these first two levels is that they are largely mechanical and can usually be fixed easily. When we move into the top three levels we experience that word again, "Feelings." Do we feel that we are loved and have a sense of belonging? Do we feel that we are recognized? Do we feel appreciated?

Depressingly a very significant proportion of the working population answers NO! to these questions. I have seen some reports that this could be as high as 60% of people at work. This represents a huge management challenge to improve its "Generic Motivation" culture.

Level four ,"Esteem," is interesting and in the idealistic world where we would like everyone to at least reach. This means that they have no day-to-day worries, feel appreciated and included and are RESPECTED (Esteem) for their contribution.

The top state of SELF-ACTUALIZATION (which is attributed to Kurt Goldstein, 1878) means that we reach our full and true potential. This is of course great in one way, but a problem in another way. Where do we go after that? Here we may have a problem?

I believe that the management challenge is to keep the targets / tasks sufficiently challenging that the Self-Actualization level is rarely reached, and when it is a new goal is given to reset the criteria for self-actualization. The reason this is required is that people who are at that top level often have time on their hands and may cause problems. They potentially become disruptive because they are usually well thought of and respected and the challenges of the job are insufficient to keep them focused on productive work. They may therefore, potentially go and cause trouble and ultimately become less effective.

An everyday example of this effect can often be seen in the sports world or the entertainment industry. Someone starts off as an unknown and starts to gain recognition and respect and moves, often quite quickly, into a powerful position. Look at some of the top TV series and watch how over the life of the series you start to see that the star become listed as the director or the producer. Then correlate that with the show losing its edge and initial attraction. It happens! Not always of course, but sufficient to make the point that SELF-ACTUALIZATION can be a destructive force. Watch it.

BULLY BOYS AND GIRLS

An interesting area and one that I have mixed views. I totally disagree with aggressive and unreasonable behavior by management. I see it as the worst possible abuse of power. Particularly when directed at people that are unable to defend themselves without losing their job. But, I have seen it work very effectively and consequently I have spent some time thinking through why the aggressive and unreasonable treatment of people should produce good results. A little conflict in my personal value system. On the one hand, I see that good behavior towards people is fundamental. On the other hand, results define success. An apparent conflict? My conclusion is that there are three areas where this works — two good ways and one not so good.

A Good One

Sometimes a business requires a shake up, change of direction, new blood, new people and an executive is recruited with a mission to do that. This involves changes and maybe some aggressive behavior. If the people get that, and they have *respect for the leader* they will accept it as being a good and necessary evolutionary stage in the business. I have been in some very aggressive situations with low pay and loved it. Because it was not personal, it was an aspect of culture and a great learning opportunity. Learn fast or go. Plus the top executives were really good and hard working and never asked for more than they were doing themselves. Respect top to bottom!

The Bad One

Take the scenario outlined in the last example, but take away the respect and add another dimension — "FEAR." This type of manager acts really aggressively, but most importantly is not respected and uses the fear of being fired as a major weapon. What usually happens is that the fear factor causes an initial lift in performance, which acts as a validation of their actions and this then feeds continuing bad behavior. The good people get it, and although they do not like the toxic environment they conform in the short term and later leave. This type of manager also often pays well as a retention tool to compensate for what is often a collapse in the Generic Motivation culture. After maybe a couple of years these managers usually move, interestingly usually to better jobs because they are able to demonstrate good results and the company they leave gives a good reference to get rid. Then the company has to be cleaned up by another manager and the heads of the people put back in place.

Another Good One

I have seen this so many times and it works. Usually a small business often with the senior person who is the owner /manager. A small team usually that have been together a long time. The manager is hands on 24/7 and knows everyone well. This manager behaves in the most unreasonable aggressive and almost psychotic way. Yet everyone loves them. Why?

Because they care passionately and just want the best. People get that and are usually prepared to put up with it. These personalities also tend to do some remarkably generous, out of character acts. Like agreeing to pay all medical expenses of a young warehouse employee and confirming that their job is safe. They care and it shows. People respect that behavior and will consequently put up with a lot. Not too much, of course.

LEAKAGE

This a term used in the study of "Body Language." Our actions, often subconscious, communicate our real feelings. The nervous twitch, the folded arms, etc. In the context of motivation I would like to widen this term out to be more generic about how people view us in the context of leaders and motivators.

A few fundamental points that require to be made. People are much wiser and smarter than people in positions of power and authority give them credit for. They can usually work out a phony pretty quickly and if you do not **REALLY CARE** they get that quickly. The way they get it is the way we leak our behavior in areas that may not be viewed as front line task. In particular, it is to do with our personal behavior. How we act and are observed will be more powerful than what we say and write. For example.

If when you are presenting or formally talking to your team all the words are correct and the language is good and motivating. Expressions like "Team Mates," "We all in together," "Really appreciate your efforts," "Great being part of this team," etc., etc., any reasonable person can string a few positive words together. But if you then do something that is totally self-serving and not in line with the speech, then you are done for.

For example, every time a problem arises your first words are, "Who is to blame? Who do we fire?"

Or maybe you use language in what you think are private meetings like "Slash and burn" or "Heads will roll." These things leak the **REAL YOU.**

Guess which way most people go?

Listen to what you say formally. "Team mates" or "Watch what you do?"

Our personal actions define what type of leader we are!

MOTIVATION — PULLING IT ALL TOGETHER

Some conclusions from all these comments and thoughts. I often muse over what the conversation would be like if the people mentioned in this section all met over dinner and talked about "Motivation." These are the notes that would probably come out of that meeting.

GENERIC MOTIVATION

We need to make sure that all our people have a good working environment and feel safe. *Herzberg*

If we ever have to tell some bad news, like a downsizing, we need to do it all at once and be open and honest. *Machiavelli*

Our managers should be trained to walk the floor and talk to people in a respectful way that makes them feel included and valuable. *Carnegie*

We require a form of regular appraisal system where we can talk to people individually about their performance and any concerns that exist from either side. *Herzberg*

We should introduce continuous improvement programs that enable everyone to feel valued and that provide an opportunity for him or her to contribute. *Hawthorne*

SPECIFIC MOTIVATION

We need a system to recognize any special achievements and make them public that will create respect. *Maslow / Herzberg*

We need to look at where each individual is on the needs hierarchy and make sure that they feel secure enough to perform, but remain tasked and challenged. *Maslow*

MOTIVATIONAL MODEL

MANAGEMENT INPUT

PAY AND CONDITIONS
COMMUNICATIONS
POSITIVE CULTURE
APPRAISAL SYSTEMS
TRUST

VISION
INCENTIVES / REWARDS
GOALS
PERFORMANCE MEASURES

INCLUSION

GENERIC MOTIVATION

NOTE

THE GREATER THE PRESENCE OF GENERIC MOTIVATION, THE LESS INPUT IS REQUIRED FOR SPECIFIC MOTIVATION PEOPLE BECOME MORE PROACTIVE / SELF-STARTING

SPECIFIC MOTIVATION

TASK FOCUSED / GETTING THINGS DONE
EFFECTIVE PERFORMANCE

AN EFFECTIVE RESULTS DRIVEN ORGANIZATION AT OPTIMUM COST

PEOPLE SKILLS

DEVELOPING PEOPLE SKILLS
EVERY DAY EXAMPLES
HUMOR
COMMUNICATIONS
WORDS WE USE
CULTURE
TEAM WORK
MOST EFFECTIVE TIP
(THAT YOU WILL BE UNABLE TO DO?)

DEVELOPING PEOPLE SKILLS

WHY IMPORTANT?

Inspiring, leading and motivating is largely an interpersonal process. How you are, what you are and how you behave is a major factor people take into account when deciding if they want to follow or support you. This is true if you are voting for the president or helping as the local Boy Scout troop leader. It is certainly true in the workplace.

WHAT ARE PEOPLE SKILLS?

A really good question. That's a good people skill right at the start. When asked a question pay respect to the questioner and the question. People skills could be defined as "The ability to relate to everyone in a positive way such that they leave you with a positive and supportive impression."

HOW DO YOU DEVELOP THEM?

This is an ongoing 24/7 task to be worked on when awake and in any form of contact with another person. Talk to anyone, anywhere and learn to relate to them. Use the "How to Win Friends and Influence People" techniques. Hidden benefits often come from this activity. See the YOGA instructor story in the appendices.

ARE YOU FIT FOR PURPOSE?

People skills come more naturally to some people than others. Maybe the charismatic socially confident person. Accepting that this is a good personal attribute it is not the defining requirement. The most important qualities are sincerity and wanting to relate to your fellow man in a positive and empathetic way. This can be achieved by all personality types. We have all seen larger than life characters that are full of it and are not to be trusted. Conversely, we have all seen quietly spoken conservative people that come across as compassionate and caring. You are what you are, but that does not preclude you from working on people skills. If you find this area really hard and have no empathy with the process then you probably should not be in the business of working with people. Maybe?

PEOPLE SKILLS. EVERY DAY EXAMPLES

This page role plays some pretty typical conversations that we all have. These conversations are intended to make a few points about how people relate to each other and hopefully draw some parallel for the workplace.

PICK A SUBJECT, ANY SUBJECT

YOU SAY. I had a terrible flight yesterday delayed nearly 5 hours.

THE SKILLED PEOPLES PERSON SAYS. How terrible did it cause you any problems? (Note the open question at the end.)

MOST PEOPLE. I had the a similar experience the other day…..etc., etc..

THE POINT
Most people when a subject is raised immediately stop really listening to you, think of something to do with them, wait for a gap in the conversation and off they go. Depending upon the situation this is good or bad news.

TALKING ABOUT YOU

YOU ARE ASKED. How are you?

THE SKILLED PEOPLES PERSON SAYS. Great thanks for asking, how are you? (Note the open question at the end.)

MOST PEOPLE. You would not believe the day that I had yesterday…..etc., etc.

THE POINT
Most people are not really interested in you so switch it back to their favorite subject THEM. You can listen for hours, say nothing and they think that you are a great person. (Listener)

SOMETHING ABOUT YOU

YOU ARE ASKED. How are the family?

THE SKILLED PEOPLES PERSON SAYS. Great thanks for asking, how are yours? (Note the open question at the end.) If you can add a personal snippet from last time like "Is your son enjoying college?" Very effective.

MOST PEOPLE. They are doing great thanks, Charlie had just graduated from dental school in the Phillipes, Sarah is about to go to Europe for a trip etc., etc., etc.…just let them go it suits you?

Of course some people are genuinely interested in you,
but you cannot keeping chatting to your mother all the time!

THE POINT
Most people ask these standard questions as conversational points and usually only interested in their own families.

**BY NOW SOME WILL THINK THAT THIS IS A CYNICAL VIEW.
NOT INTENDED AS SUCH, JUST A COMMENT ON THE NATURE OF PEOPLE.
IF YOU HAVE ANY DOUBTS JUST START A FEW CONVERSATIONS
AND FORGET YOUR AGENDA.**

OBSERVE AND LISTEN

HUMOR

THE IN CROWD
One of the bosses that I used to work with used to say to someone that had just made a mistake one of two expressions. Either "How long have you been with us, not counting today?" or "That's a funny way to hand in your notice." To a switched-on, highly-motivated team that are confident with each other and recognize that the odd mistake is inevitable that was funny. How we laughed!

HOWEVER
To the wrong person in the wrong place for the wrong reasons, these same words could cause great offence and in extreme cases lead to some type of lawsuit for harassment or bullying. Especially if not delivered with a smile.

THE CONCLUSION
**Humor can be an incredibly powerful bonding experience,
but it has serious dangers.**

THE BENEFITS OF HUMOR
Can break the ice and relax people.

Can defuse a tense situation.

Can make you seem normal and human.

You can make serious point in a non-confrontational way.

It can be a bonding factor relating to shared experiences.

THE RISKS WITH HUMOR
It may not travel well across cultures.

It could lead to a feeling of exclusion if "in jokes" are used.

Not everyone who thinks that they are funny really are.

It can be difficult to retract from a comment once launched.

It can lead to misinterpretation.

The politically correct and legal agenda is a minefield for bad jokes.

HOWEVER, I COULD NOT RESIST THIS ONE
I was involved in a very tense 3 day dispute with the trade unions in Liverpool (UK) well known for the Beatles and its difficult labor relations. We were getting nowhere and the Union was just about to call a walk out, which would have cost us about $3M a day in lost production. The dispute was about an apparently inadequate heating system. Matters were getting tense when in the middle of a heated argument one of the shop stewards said, "You call that heating? It would not melt the dick of a chocolate mouse." Everyone was convulsed in laughter literally not being able to speak for a while. How could you carry on the aggression after that? Dispute settled in 30 minutes all back to work. True story.

IF IN ANY DOUBT WHAT SO EVER.   LEAVE IT OUT AND KEEP IT STRAIGHT.

COMMUNICATIONS

KEY QUESTIONS BEFORE COMMUNICATING

What do I want to say?

Who to?

What do I want them to do?

How will I know if it has been successful?

From my observations considerable effort is put into answering the first question. Not much effort into the subsequent questions, especially the last one. How will I know if it has been successful? Which is unfortunate as a more rigorous assessment of the last three questions will often determine a better answer to the first question. "What do I want to say? We are so frequently in transmit mode only (Que 1) with little or no thought to the consequences of our communications. We often do not ask if we are achieving a positive result or indeed if we are generating a negative reaction.

WHAT IS COMMUNICATION?

The other major aspect of basic communications is to define "What is communication?" The answer is quite simple, especially for a leader. It starts with just a presence. How we look, walk, behave, our body language are all sending communication signals before we even speak! When we speak and whatever we say this is clearly communication. The casual comment or remark will define us for so many people, often more than formal communication. Speeches, presentations, correspondence, etc.

HOW DO WE COMMUNICATE?

Our actions define us as people and especially as leaders. People watch what we do. People do not always listen to what we say. The two most important impacts we have on a person are how we treat them with our actions and how we make them feel. Much more relevant than what we say. Clever talking is very unlikely to correct any serious mistakes in these two areas.

TECHNOLOGY

A word of warning. Modern technology provides spectacular and instant communication. Often worldwide with the press of a few buttons. Most of which can not be easily UNDONE and it could haunt you forever. Make sure that the basics of what you want to achieve are very well thought out and that you do not fall in love with the technology, which is just a tool.

WORDS WE USE

The way you conduct yourself is very important to how people will relate to both you and more importantly, the business. Motivation, engagement and how we feel are all influenced by a variety of factors one of which is our communication.
This page shows some of the words that we use, the GOOD words that have a positive impact and BAD words that have a negative effect. The more senior the position you hold and the less frequently that you may see someone on a personal level, then the more important these relatively small sound bites become.
Words require to be chosen very carefully.

GOOD WORDS

Thank you / Can you help me please? / What do you think? / What is your name? (not every time you meet!) / How long have you been here? / I appreciate all that you are doing for me / Your manager just told me what a great job you are doing (especially if the manager didn't!!) / How are the family? Ball team? etc., or any other interests? / That's great input, thanks / Good job

BAD WORDS

Go away, I am too busy / I don't care / Who are you again? / Are you stupid or what? / I hear what you say (but I am not really interested) / Who do you think that you are? / Get out of my way / Nothing to do with you / So I hear (but who cares) / That is none of your business.

WORST OF ALL……NO WORDS

CULTURE

A huge and complex subject, but very important in the workplace. A business includes many people that may have come from many cultures outside. Obvious ones like race and religion and less obvious ones that reside in the value system of an individual. The job in the workplace is to bring all these many cultures together and focus them in a "work related culture" that is specific to the requirements of the business.

This is a huge and important role of the person at the top to set the cultural tone of the business. The starting point, in my view, is to set the standards for your own personal behavior that you want the rest of the organization to follow. Lead by example. Set the right "Tone from the Top."

Nothing is more important in setting the culture of an organization than "The way it treats its people." This has to be the touchstone for integrity and recognizing performance. Because this area is so fundamentally important a few ideas on how to ensure that the organization is developing and operating to the culture that you require and how you think it is working.

- Become personally involved in key people decisions.
- Introduce and review "Exit Interviews" find out why people have left. Talk to them personally if it is important. Do not leave it to HR.
- If people have to be let go, treat them fairly and with respect. The rest of the organization will be watching. Plus you never know where the person will end up. Could be with your largest customer.
- Pay attention to areas that people think are important that you may not. Like eating arrangements, bathroom cleanliness. These are signs of how the company thinks.
- Develop a formal and regular communication plan. Not just wait until bad news has to be imparted.

TONE FROM THE TOP VERY IMPORTANT

TEAMWORK

The purpose of TEAM is create an output that is greater than the individual parts.

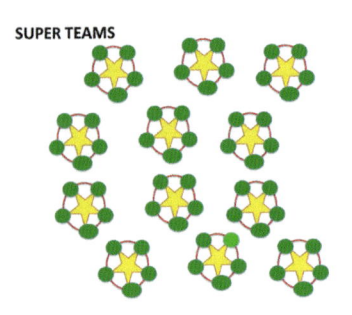

SUPER TEAMS

These are the teams where all the KEY AREAS are aligned. They consequently have a strong LIFE FORCE and the SPECIFIC MOTIVATION is collectively focused.

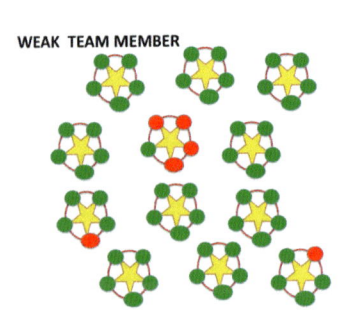

WEAK TEAM MEMBER

No team is perfect. The challenge for the TEAM and its leader is to find out where the weak links are. Then to either correct them through training or replace them. Meanwhile the rest of the TEAM has to develop techniques to cover this hopefully isolated weakness.

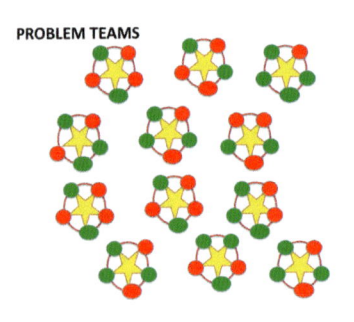

PROBLEM TEAMS

This is a major challenge that requires STRUCTURAL ATTENTION. For this number of team members to have this amount of KEY AREAS going down something is wrong with the structure, not the individual team members.
Find out what it is and put it right.

KEY POINTS FOR TEAM BUILDING

Create a balanced multi-skilled TEAM.

Look for strong working together skills.

PEOPLE SKILLS

A REALLY USEFUL TIP THAT YOU WILL IGNORE

We all talk about each other behind each others backs, good and bad. Not everyone likes everyone and the nature of people is that negative and bad views are usually more interesting. ("There is something not too displeasing about the misfortunes of our friends....." ~William Shakespeare)

> **Never say anything bad about anybody, any time, anywhere to anybody.**

There are absolutely never any upsides from sending negative comments out. Never.

WHY?

The person that you are talking to may go away and think. What do you say about them behind their back? You could get a reputation for being negative.

The person that you are talking about will usually get to hear about it.

Negative thoughts deplete your own emotional energy. Move on, be positive.

A professional executive is not paid to like everyone, or they like you. You are however paid to behave professionally towards everyone on the payroll or connected with the business.

If the person thinks equally the same about you. Which they often do. If they hear that you have said something positive about them, they may well become a supporter.

> **This is probably the single biggest people skill that you could develop. Will you?**
> **NOT A CHANCE!!**

ROAD BLOCKS

EGO / PRIDE / EMOTIONS / PREJUDICES / STUBBORNNESS / ACCEPTING WE MAY BE WRONG

REALLY GREAT QUALITIES TO REALIZE THAT YOU HAVE?

ENERGY

PHYSICAL ENERGY

We require a basic level of PHYSICAL FITNESS AND INTELLIGENCE in order to do the job. Leaders have a particular responsibility to the team to stay fit. Plus it sends a message. If a person is unable to look after their most valuable possession, their own body, then why should I trust them to look after anything else?

EMOTIONAL ENERGY

There is a major crossover and interdependency between our **EMOTIONS** and how the impact our **ENERGY**. It can sometimes be difficult to separate the cause and effect in people. Leaders require to be aware of how these areas relate and impact how we perform.

EMOTIONS

We all have emotions and feelings. Everyone has the good ones and the bad ones. It is just a matter of degree and how well we control them and how we let them effect what we do and say. We should TRY and develop the good ones and mitigate or reduce the impact of the bad ones.

THE BAD ONES
ANGER / JEALOUSY / JUDGMENTAL / DEPRESSED / WORRY / GUILT / HATE / FEAR

THE GOOD ONES
CARE / LOVE / COMPASSION / UNDERSTANDING / RESPECT / PATIENCE / HAPPINESS

TO CONTROL EMOTIONS IS REALLY HARD, BUT WE DO NEED TO BE AWARE OF THEIR IMPACT AND TRY NOT TO ALLOW THEM TO AFFECT OUR JUDGMENT AND ACTIONS IN THE WORKPLACE. DIFFICULT. WELCOME TO THE HUMAN RACE.

LIFE FORCE RECAP

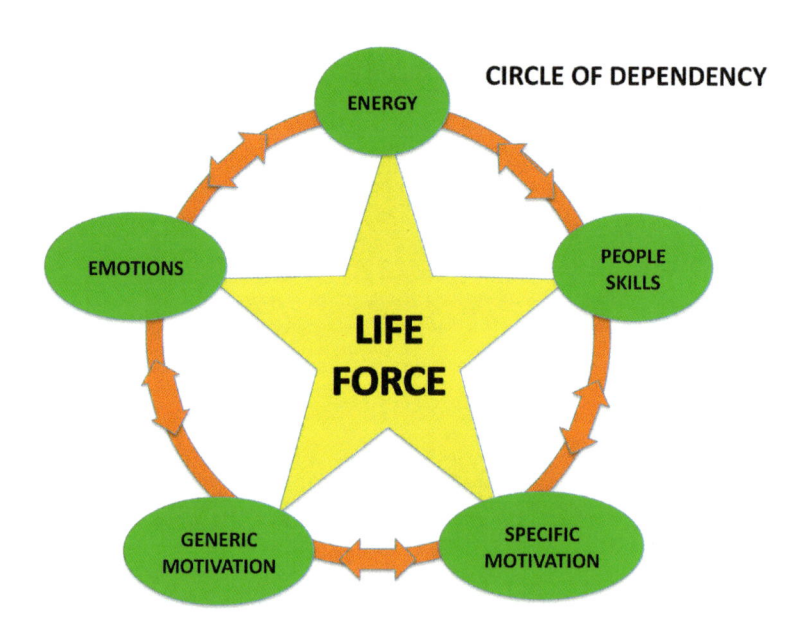

CIRCLE OF DEPENDENCY

- ENERGY
- PEOPLE SKILLS
- SPECIFIC MOTIVATION
- GENERIC MOTIVATION
- EMOTIONS

LIFE FORCE

CHECK LIST

Make sure that the 5 KEY AREAS are all functioning and OK for **YOU**.

Review your team against the 5 KEY AREAS.

Look for any issues within the team that are impacting performance as a result of issues in the 5 KEY AREAS.

Review the actions that strengthen the 5 KEY AREAS. Develop actions and training programs to build strength in you and the team.

Watch for **LIFE FORCE DEPLETION**. This is serious.

RELATED SUBJECTS

LEADERSHIP v. MANAGEMENT

LEADER

Focuses more on vision, direction and inspiration.

COLLABORATES / PERSUADES

RELATIONSHIPS

INSPIRES

GAINS RESPECT / COMMITMENT

FACILITATES ON PROBLEM SOLVING

GOALS DRIVEN BY DESIRE

SELF EVALUATES

HIGH EMOTIONAL INTELLIGENCE

MANAGER

Focuses more on task, execution and getting things done.

There are of course good and bad managers and all good managers have strong leadership qualities that enable them to be effective. Pure management can however lead to some extreme behavior, which has to be guarded against, including.

TRIES TO BE TOO CONTROLLING

ORDERS OTHERS, DICTATES

INSTILLS FEARS

USES POSITIONAL POWER

SOLVES PROBLEMS DRIVEN BY PERSONAL NEED

RELIES ON IQ & INTELLIGENCE

BUSINESS EXECUTIVE / GENERAL MANAGER

Part Leader, part Manager. A Question of balance?

Where do you line up?

LEADERSHIP SKILLS CAN BE GAINED. WORK ON THEM.

BRINGING IT ALL TOGETHER

THE LEADER'S CHALLENGE
Review everyone on an individual basis

Do they have a clear brief of what is expected of them?

Do they have clear goals set with measures and incentives to achieve?

Are their hygiene factors OK? Are they unhappy about anything?

Where are they on the Maslow hierarchy?
Is the job too much, too little?

Increase or decrease load, as required.

Do they have the right training to do the job?

Do they have a contract that reflects their role and importance?

Do they have a regular review and opportunity
to discuss performance?

Have you given them a vision of where they could
develop to if successful?

Can they do more, have you asked them?

Are they stressed? Have you asked them? Have you checked?

How is their team performing?

Make them feel special and unique.

Are they passing down and spreading these points to others?

HOW TO BE A GOOD BOSS / LEADER

*This is work in progress a continuing learning experience.
But the story so far.*

ACCEPT PERSONAL RESPONSIBILITY FOR THE FOLLOWING

That the business makes money and does not run out of cash.
That the business has a plan / mission and is constantly improved to survive.
That you remain fit and able to do your job.

IF YOU FAIL ON THESE THREE KEY OBJECTIVES, GAME OVER!

YOU and / or THE BUSINESS will not be here!

THEN

A DYNAMIC ORGANIZATION
The organization you lead is made up of people all with feelings, aspirations, different life experiences and different skills. It is a dynamic living entity that requires constant attention. An organization does not perform as the rigid organization chart would indicate. Not even close.

BE A ROLE MODEL
Make sure that your personal behavior is creating the right impressions. How you are defines you. YOU define your personal qualities as a LEADER.
A 24/7 constant work in progress task.

RESPECT EVERYONE
Treat everyone with equal respect as a valuable member of the team. Tell them.

YOU ARE A PERSON
Understand your own strengths, weaknesses and prejudices. Ensure that they do not impact your judgment and decision making. Remain OBJECTIVE. You will also have to keep some of your doubts and fears to yourself. The team expect certainty from leaders. This is unrealistic but understand it. **LEADERSHIP CAN BE LONELY.**

ACCEPT YOUR LIMITATIONS
You are not GOD and you cannot solve everybody's problems. Sometimes you just have to leave people to get on with things, or to get over something. Time and patience may be required. Many issues do have a tendency to work themselves out naturally.

HOW TO BE A GOOD BOSS / LEADER

NOT MANAGE EVERYONE THE SAME WAY
In some areas it is important that everyone feels that they are treated as equals and fairly. However, we are all different and have different abilities and skills and also have different expectations from the workplace. This requires to be recognized and everyone given an individual path to follow. Providing of course this is realistic with the constraints and requirements of the business.

BE A MENTOR / BE APPROACHABLE
What I have found as I progressed up the ladder is that the clever stuff — strategy, financial analysis, decision making, etc. — tends to be the weekend thinking time. Contact time with the organization should be viewed as an opportunity to inspire and mentor. People are interested in getting on and finding out about new and interesting experiences. If you are able to just sit down with some one once in a while, it will help. Guess what, it is not only that person that will benefit, the team will notice and hopefully respect your interest. Just avoid focusing on favorites.

REPEAT AND BE BORING
Do have a few sound bites that define your management style and communicate your value system. Some of my favorites: "The limitation to progress lies between your ears." "Go for it, you can do this." "So do it NOW." People need to be constantly reminded of these culturally defining points. Use them often.

INSPIRE
Be creative, Inject energy. Lift people's vision. Let them know on a regular basis that they can achieve so much more. That you will help them. Plus, also let them know that the odd mistake along the way is fine. Performance is about averages.

HAVE FUN
You spend a lot of time at work try and make it as enjoyable as possible. The best performing teams that I have worked with have been full of humor and energy. A virtuous circle with success. This is also an antidote to FEAR, which is usually very TOXIC in any organization.

POWER & POLITICS

DEFINITIONS

Power is required to get anything done. Therefore, it is important to understand what POWER you have and also what POWER may be working against you.

TYPES OF POWER

POSITIONAL
(Your job title and responsibilities)

INFORMATION
(Knowledge is power)

WEALTH
(Money speaks and usually is listened to!)

KNOWLEDGE & RESPECT
(The Go to Person that is respected)

PHYSICAL
(Brute force physical strength)

BUSINESS POLITICS

Most people are relatively ambitious and they equate success with moving up in an organization and becoming more powerful. The issue is how to do this? Ideally this should be on excellent performance and the ability to manage well. In small companies this is probably true as it is fairly obvious. For the larger organizations, the definition of excellent performance is difficult to identify. This is particularly true in a process rich environment with a lot of people with nebulous targets to meet, therefore people skills in gaining support become more effective. The cynical label attached to this is politics. Many of the well-paid powerful positions in large organizations are so far removed from the performance of the business that these political skills become much more evident and they can be very debilitating for an organization.

UNDER-RATED LEADERSHIP SKILLS

These are some of the things that a good leader should do. If effective, they will largely go unnoticed. As they should.

1. Keeping quiet
2. Letting someone else take the credit
3. Forego personal reward for the benefit of the team
4. Spend core time with the team and do your personal work out of hours
5. Watch everyone talk and just let them get on with it. If you agree?
6. Not change things just because you are the boss and you can
7. Letting someone see a weakness once in a while
8. Not take yourself too seriously
9. Fix a problem for someone anonymously. In and out of work
10. Let someone go ahead and make a mistake as a learning experience. Not a big one!
11. Not using positional power thoughtlessly
12. Accepting that you were wrong
13. Apologizing. Quickly and up front. Always best
14. Avoiding the temptation to say "I told you so"
15. Pretending that the Board are doing a good job. Really difficult
16. Keeping out the way and letting people get on with the job
17. Avoiding the words "Good and Bad" and "Right and Wrong" when changing things. Just different

ORGANIZATION STRUCTURES AND CHARTS

This section deals with how businesses try to represent the way the organization works on paper in a two dimensional format. Even that first sentence should be a clue that I am not a big fan of organization charts.

Before we start to demolish the whole concept of organization charts, a few points;

It is essential that every person knows where they fit into organization, who they report to, who reports to them and what is expected from them.

The issue is "Are organization charts the best way to achieve that?"

SOMETHING TO CONSIDER

An exercise that I have done as preparation to talk to an MBA group is to obtain all their names and construct an organization chart. Classic pyramid, nothing fancy like a matrix chart. I select someone for the top box, miss a few people out, deliberately misspell a few names. When the time comes I put the chart up and ask a few questions.

Where did you first look? To find your own name?
What did you think when it was not there? (usually 10%)
Why do you think that person was put in the top box?
Is the person in the top box happy to be there?
How do you feel that your name has been spelled wrongly?
How do all those people on the bottom level feel?

The conclusion: Most people in the room are not happy with the chart.

The point: The only person normally OK with an organization chart is the person in the top box. So why take the risk of upsetting so many people by making it so obvious that they are well down the league table of importance. Everyone in an organization is required and is important. There are much better ways of explaining where people fit in than an organization chart.

THE GOOD USES

I fully accept that organizations do require charts to show where the people are supposed to be. This is **useful for outsiders** to get up to speed quickly on who fits in where and what they are supposed to do. Especially for say a quality audit. Just do not use them as a dynamic management tool. They tell more people what they cannot do rather than can do. Never a good idea to limit a persons' perception of their own importance.

I AM NOT REALLY INTERESTED IN DISCUSSING THE VARIOUS OTHER CHARTS.
THESE POINTS APPLY TO ALL OF THEM.

THE LAW

IMPORTANT THIS CAN COST A LOT OF MONEY

Managers are increasingly having to deal with an increasing load of regulations and laws. The ability to act without reference to a specialist, like a lawyer is diminishing on a daily basis. The laws surrounding the employment of people are many and various and range from the good and required to what in my view are trivial and ridiculous. This book is not intended to provide a lengthy analysis of all the various laws and regulations that apply to the workplace, but you do need to know that there are a lot of them and they are increasing in complexity and frequency. The other point to be aware of is that different countries have different laws and regulations, so when dealing internationally make sure that you take expert device on the local laws and if any of them can be flowed back to your home country. So a few popular areas that you require to be aware of.

AREAS THAT CAN RESULT IN LEGAL ACTIONS

Discrimination at any level, race, religion, sex, etc.

Unfair termination of employment.

Not observing standard hours of work and overtime.

Not providing a safe working environment and adequate safety protection equipment.

Not carrying out medical tests when working in hazardous areas.

Illegally using employees funds, like the pension scheme.

Trade union law and agreements.

Infringing basic human rights. (Court of human rights in Europe.)

Transferring the rights of companies when taken over.

Closing / moving a business if it is profitable. (European countries check it out.)

REMEMBER MOST OF THE LEGISLATION FAVORS THE INDIVIDUAL, NOT THE CORPORATION

This is a highly specialized area and it will be impossible for the average GM to keep totally up-to-date. If you plan to do anything substantial in this area take advice. Make sure that the HR department is also keeping up with the current legislation.

PEOPLE IN HIGH PLACES

SOME SHARED EXPERIENCES

I have had the pleasure of meeting quite a few people in so called "High Places," including some people that would be well-known. I thought that I would share some of these interesting experiences. No names, of course. Some personal observations.

Most of the people are nice, friendly and very approachable. The problem is to get past "their people," who can quite often be the exact opposite. But if you can establish a direct contact, it will usually be more productive than you may think.

The people that you read about as the "Captains of Industry" are a very small minority of the hard working and regular CEOs that are just getting on with the job. Talented as these icons may or may not be, this is the show business branch of corporate life.

A minority of these well-known people have egos of the scale and behave in the most incredible way imaginable. They should be avoided.

Being a successful top executive has a lot to do with factors like "Who you know," "Being in the right place at the right time," "Luck catching a good market." To get to this elevated status I believe that you have to have something going for you. This is not always ability and intelligence, which are not a perfect correlation for power.

If you work for a small company and a have a large business as your customer, then there is a tendency to want to go and see the top executive. Just be warned this is not always a good an idea as you may think. Why? Because if they have never met you before he could well ask their people (your contacts) to prepare a paper or two about you and your company which causes them more work. Not happy. They also could be annoyed that you have by passed their authority. The other danger is that if you represent a group with several companies, they may not be totally visible as a total entity to the top person. A visit could trigger interest and a request for a discount because of the business volumes. Happened to me, a very expensive meeting.

SELF-HELP BOOKS

This page could save you a lot of reading

As one of my hero's would say, the title is a good start. It's not self-help, if you require a book. It's HELP. The vast majority of these books are based on a few principles, which if you have the self-discipline to follow, then you do not need to read another self-help book except to remain topical. This is more of a "fashion" industry than you may realize.

SELF-HELP TIPS

YOU are the only person that can fix YOU.

Watch what you eat and drink.

Take exercise and look after your weight and blood pressure.

Get an annual physical that checks for the basic things.

Be nice to people and treat them with respect.

Realize that you can do more than you probably think.

Be realistic about your expectations.

Do not be judgmental.

Socialize and be happy.

Laugh. Especially at yourself. A very funny subject usually.

Be a responsible citizen and member of the human race.

Try and have BALANCE in your life.

Live within your financial means. Watch debt. Especially credit cards.

Do not take yourself too seriously.

If some form of spiritual activity works for YOU, do it.

Respect other persons views, beliefs and spiritual persona.

Try and live in the NOW.

BY THE WAY, THIS IS NOT A SELF-HELP BOOK. IT IS A COLLECTION OF OPINIONS ON HOW PEOPLE REACT IN THE WORKPLACE.

SELLING & NEGOTIATION

Two huge subjects on which a lot of material exists to study them. This book is about people, so all I would like to do is to make a few points about both of these subjects in the context of "People Management."

Sales and Negotiating skills are relevant to all walks of life.
They are basic life skills. Everyone should be encouraged to attend
some formal training in these areas.

These skills are required in many of the people-related activities in a business in addition to the sales process including: applying for a job, getting people to do things, annual pay reviews and trade union relations.

Understand that both of these activities are ongoing processes, not events.
Our behavior is a constant process of selling ourselves. How we behave also
"conditions" people that we may have to negotiate with what
the likely outcome may be.

MEASURING THE PRODUCTIVITY AND COST OF PEOPLE

PEOPLE COSTS

Mission check. The manager's job is to gain maximum performance at OPTIMUM COST, so we need to make sure that is being achieved. Therefore, it is important to find out what the actual cost of employing people is. Then compare these costs (opposite page) to the results of the business.

EASY COSTS TO MEASURE

The easiest costs to measure are the ones that you actually pay out either DIRECTLY to the person or paid indirectly on their behalf. These include:

Direct payroll, including overtime and bonuses

Government / state taxes and insurances

Travelling expenses

Medical and other insurances

Pension contributions

THE OVERHEAD COSTS OF EMPLOYING PEOPLE IS VERY HIGH. MEASURE IT

HIDDEN COSTS OF PEOPLE

People who are badly trained and motivated can also cost the business vast amounts of money. This can result in the failure of the business if for example, a massive fraud becomes terminal. Some examples of how people cost money in a bad way.

Theft / pilferage / fraud / unauthorized use of company resources

Inefficiency / incompetent behavior / scrap

Selling or giving away information

Upsetting and losing customers

Absence / time wasting / poor influence

Breaking the law

THESE ARE IMPORTANT ISSUES. WATCH OUT FOR THEM AND PUT CONTROLS IN

MEASURING THE PRODUCTIVITY AND COST OF PEOPLE

THE APPROACH

ESTABLISH ACTUAL COSTS
CREATE SOME KPIs (KEY PERFORMANCE INDICATORS OR RATIOS)
INVESTIGATE VARIANCES TO BUDGET OR COST / PERFORMANCE DRIFT
IF ABSORPTION COSTING IS USED MAKE SURE THAT THE STANDARDS ARE REVIEWED

See the A DAY WITH A CEO book on FINANCE for more details.

SOME TYPICAL RATIOS TO MEASURE PEOPLE COSTS

A RATIO is created by dividing two or numbers into each other to produce one number.
The RATIO can stand alone as fact, but more usually for comparison reasons
Compared to either trends within the business
OR
To compare with other companies to produce a comparative measure (Peer group comp)
A RATIO is a specific type of KPI

PRODUCTIVITY
SALES PER PERSON = $\dfrac{\text{TOTAL SALES}}{\text{HEAD COUNT}}$ — **HIGHER BETTER**

COST
COST PER PERSON = $\dfrac{\text{TOTAL PAYROLL}}{\text{HEAD COUNT}}$ — **LOWER BETTER**

ABSENCE
% LOST TIME = $\dfrac{\text{LOST DAYS}}{\text{TOTAL AVAILABLE DAYS}}$ — **LOWER BETTER**

THE HIGHER THE BETTER

PROFITABILITY
$\dfrac{\text{NET PROFIT}}{\text{HEAD COUNT}}$ — **HIGHER BETTER**

TO CHECK RETURN ON SALES

PAYROLL DRIFT
HIDDEN COSTS = $\dfrac{\text{ACTUAL COST PER PERSON}}{\text{BUDGET COST PER PERSON}}$

PRODUCTIVITY
$\dfrac{\text{PEOPLE OVERHEAD COSTS}}{\text{DIRECT PAYROLL COSTS}}$ — **LOWER BETTER**

**MANY MORE RATIOS EXIST OR CAN BE CREATED
MAKE SURE THAT YOU SELECT OR DESIGN THE MOST APPROPRIATE
ONES FOR YOUR BUSINESS
IDEALLY A RATIO SHOULD RESULT IN THE HIGHER THE
NUMBER THE BETTER?**

MANAGING THE BOSS

The first task is to establish who your boss is. To start you could look at one of those mickey mouse organization charts, find your name, follow the hopefully ONE unbroken line up the chart and the name in the next box is your boss. If only life was that simple!

You need to work out who has the power to influence your destiny with regard to you remaining employed in your current job.

This can be one of, or all of the following.

Anyone in the business, including those below you.
They may know people in high places.

Customers. They can certainly get you fired.

Board members who pay attention.

Official bodies / law. You break them you may get fired or locked up.

Significant people in your personal life, husband, wife, partner, children, parents. They may all influence if you stay in your job and maybe how you do it.

Influential people anywhere that know any of the above.

YOU. Make sure you remain fit for purpose.

HOW DO YOU KEEP THEM ALL HAPPY?

For the people in the organization it should be performance and getting results, and it may well be. But what they really want is for you to **"Make them look good and not be a problem."** Just hold that thought and extrapolate it to all the people on the list. I could list many of the ways of how to do that, but that would probably take a few thousand pages and guess what it will have changed by the time it was finished. Just be aware of the need and wherever you can "Make people look good and don't be a problem."
It works at so many levels in and out of the world of work.
Make them **FEEL** good as well, that always helps.

15 / 70 / 15 Analysis

THE SITUATION

In any group of people, approximately 15% would be expected to be top performers, 70% average performers and 15% poor performers. Percentages may vary, but you no doubt get the point. Each of these groups requires to be treated slightly differently. It is also an area where you have to discipline yourself to do the right thing for the organization. Management should in my view, do the exact opposite of what instinctively actually happens. Let me explain. The area to focus on most is the 70% of the population because increased productivity from this group will give the best "TOTAL RETURN." The second area to focus on is the bottom 15% worst performers as they are a drain on the business and could be causing serious damage. The top 15% should receive minimum attention just guidance and they should largely be left alone to do what they do best. However, in my experience this seems to be the opposite way round. We tend to spend time with the top performers because it is more fun, after all they are more like us. We tend to take the 70% for granted and leave them alone to get on with it, and the bottom 15% involves some seriously unpleasant tasks, so we wait until the situation becomes critical and we are forced to deal with it.

DEALING WITH DIFFICULT PEOPLE

> *I do not have much relevant experience in this area. Sorry!*

HAVE A LOOK IN THE MIRROR?

PROTECTING PEOPLE'S TIME
(Mainly from you!)

Let me ask you to picture everyone in your team having 40 hours available each week and that every hour costs $100 each. Then imagine them walking in every Monday with 40 $100 bills in their hand. Then for every thing that you ask them to do they have to give up a $100 dollar bill for each hour they spend doing it. For example, if you call a meeting for 20 people that lasts say 2 hours and as they leave everyone puts $200 on the table. You are faced with a $4000 cost and a question. Was that value for money?

These great people that you work with and love and spend a lot of time motivating and making feel good (all of which I totally agree with) are expensive. So make sure that those $100 bills are effectively used.

NOT FOR THE FAINT HEARTED

These two pages are a little tongue in cheek and controversial. Maybe some of the thoughts will upset one or two readers, and if you have paid for the book I am sorry, but we do not have a refund policy. (See book on Finance and how to make money!) The whole point of these two pages is to make you think, maybe differently about some of the activities that we spend a lot of those $100 bills on. Maybe without thinking.
A key role of the top leader is to "Influence thinking." So think! Some examples of activities that can waste time.

S. W. O. T. Analysis

A huge waste of time most of which is spent deciding which heading a point should be allocated to. I must have seen literally hundreds of S.W.O.T.s and also spent a lot of time on the exercise. Always a good starter for the budgeting process. I cannot remember a single instance where some form of creative light went of in a S.W.O.T. exercise that really helped the business.

LOOKING AT ACQUISITIONS

Management can spend a lot of time chasing possibilities. Talking to all the people that have this great idea for your company. The success rate for these talks actually coming to something is in the very low single digit percentages. Often these discussions are interesting and the people involved smart and good to be with.
But keep focused on how much time that you and your team is spending on these discussions, the majority of which go nowhere.

PROTECTING PEOPLE'S TIME
(Mainly from you!)

THE ANNUAL BUDGET

A totally flawed concept and an almost totally irrelevant activity for a modern dynamic business in a rapidly changing world. Most businesses budget for one year ahead in detail. The process often starts maybe in Month 7 and takes probably the rest of the year to complete and get signed off. It is not unusual to get the budget actually signed off in Month 1 of the New Year, as it requires to be updated with the closing ACTUAL balances. So think about it. Depending upon where you are in the year, your use of the budget has a visibility of maybe a few weeks if you are in Month 12, or best case if you are in month 8 and have a plan you could have 20 months visibility (if you plan a full next year in Month 8 of the current year). How ridiculous is that for a tolerance.

Just to be clear, financial planning is absolutely required and fundamental to the business. This is best achieved with a rolling forecast within the real ability for the business to change. For most companies this is three or four quarters time horizon, for a company supplying large capital goods this will probably be longer. I accept that a budget is required for outsiders like banks investors, etc. Just make sure that the organization is not burning a lot of hours on what is extensive and often wasteful activity.

DO YOU GET THE THOUGHT PROCESS? ANY OTHER ACTIVITIES TO ADD?

PERFORMANCE REVIEWS?
SUCCESSION PLANNING?
?
?

GOOD OUT COMES FROM THESE SITUATIONS

Leadership is about engagement, enjoyment is about feeling included, bonding is about getting together and creating team spirit. Any activity, any activity I repeat, where you get the team in the same room to discuss a subject, any subject, is good. If the meeting is run well and not too long that people lose the will to live. So why not just meet and talk about some really interesting things as against all this boring stuff. Remember, sitting alone in your office behind closed doors is not leading. You are probably just dreaming up even more ways to waste the time of your team. An email with loads of people copied asking for some information is a good one if you must. (Please don't.)
Do something wacky once in a while, the team will love it!

CONCLUDING THOUGHTS

PERFORMANCE

A word that is frequently used, so I thought I would spend some time discussing it. What does it mean? The word is usually used to explain how a person is doing with respect to the attainment of some goals. A good performance means doing well and a poor performance means doing badly. We seem to recognize good and bad performers almost by instinct, which of course can be the first issue. Our instincts may be well developed and largely accurate, but they may not always be right. We are subject to being effected by interpersonal reactions, emotions, feelings and prejudices. It is therefore important that when we define in a managerial context performance it is accurately measured against specific targets. Avoid the "Halo Effect" of just thinking that people we like, and are maybe like us, are automatically doing well. Be objective.

Another aspect of performance measurement is that it is based on averages not 100% success. People will make mistakes, I certainly have, and anyone that does not make mistakes is in far too a comfortable a place and is not challenged. We learn by mistakes and this improves our performance average.

When reviewing the performance of people responsible for leading and managing other people the views of those people are important. You also have to look at maybe some judgmental parts of their character and integrity, quite frankly are they fit to be in charge of people. I know quite a few really intelligent, goal orientated, high achievers who should never, ever be responsible for people. They just don't get them, their often superior intelligence gets in the way of the "ordinary and often mundane" skills required to keep a team engaged and motivated. Not everyone however talented and successful should be responsible for other people.

Here we have a small issue because in the traditional business world pay and status is determined by "Positional Power," and this is usually a senior job and consequently has an organization under it. The conditioning that we are all victims of. Some people need to be put a situation on their own with specific solitary tasks and left to get on with it. Even if this results in paying them a load of money because they are very valuable contributors to the business. High intelligence and people skills are not usually highly correlated.

PERFORMANCE

A key requirement of managing people is the requirement to "manage everyone differently." An area that these contrasts show themselves is in performance reviews, especially the formal ones. When reviewing a person you not only require to be objective about the results (preferably with numbers in them), but you have to take a view on the personality of the person being reviewed. Are they optimistic, pessimistic, just doing enough to get by, etc.? Whatever the answer, you will have to adopt slightly different strategies especially when setting new goals. The optimist has to be talked down into a real and achievable goals and the pessimist talked up and stretched and maybe encouraged.

The personality of a leader, regardless of their people skills, can affect company results. For example, when I have been responsible for a group of companies for more than 3 years a trend can be determined especially when setting budgets. Manager A always just misses the budget but had a stretched and optimistic target, where as Manager B always beat budget by a small percentage because they were more street wise and made sure the budget was achievable. People skills are evident as they are managing the boss.

One of the other aspects of performance that I have observed is what I call "The trap of conformity." Let me explain. In a large corporation that has a fairly stable business and expects say 5% growth, next year this target would be communicated to the subsidiary profit owners and they then prepare the budget.

> Manager A puts in a budget showing 5% and actually achieves 6%, meets all his targets and has maximum bonus.
>
> Manager B puts in a target for 10% and achieves 8%, misses all the targets and does not get any bonus.
>
> Guess which manager is considered to be the best.

Right, Manager A. Ticks all the main boxes of corporate life, which works for so many companies. Despite manger B achieving the better performance.

KEY POINTS
Performance should be about meeting well-defined targets, ideally numerate.
Be objective and focused on the measures. Not personality likes, dislikes.
Understand it is about averages. Not 100% success all the time.
Make sure that the goals are realistic and achievable.

DIFFICULT DECISIONS THAT DEFINE AN ORGANIZATION

THE SITUATION

Once in a while a decision is required that on the face of it may not be in the best economic interests of the business. Nowhere is this more true than in the area of "PEOPLE DECISIONS" the LEADER sometimes has to make a decision because it is the "RIGHT THING TO DO." This is especially important for the leader as these decisions may require some of the business systems to be overridden. For example, I was faced with a long-serving employee that had developed a terminal illness and unfortunately had a short while to live. I discussed the situation with the person and her manager. For a variety of reasons she wanted to stay working as long as possible but on reduced hours. We agreed a plan that we all three thought "was the right thing to do." The agreement broke a few HR policies and I was actually reported to the Board Internal Audit Chairman by the internal auditor. I refused to discuss the matter and said that is what has been agreed. I would have probably resigned over the issue if it came to it. The numbers involved were very small.

THE JUSTIFICATION

This was the right thing to do and some organizations follow these policies and rules too rigidly. I think perversely the rule that I broke was one that I put in and that I had the authority to change as CEO, so clearly all a load of nonsense. Just someone following the procedures and doing their job. As they thought. My thoughts on the situation were as follows. I do not want to work with an organization that does not treat people faced with the worst moments of their life with compassion. More importantly, I do not want the rest of the organization to think that. Some would argue that this was a charitable act. I totally disagree. It is business decision to build and sustain a positive culture in the organization. It is the cost of making people want to work in this company because they "TREAT PEOPLE RIGHT." Sometimes you have to stand alone as the leader and do the right things. These decisions define you and the value system of the organization.

POWER OF BELIEF

WHAT WE DO NOT KNOW

This is the section about believe systems, faith and some things that are unexplainable by pure logic. I start with my barber, not the usual type of barber, he has hundreds of books about religion, ethics, morality, philosophy and a myriad of other related subjects. Chatting one day, I asked him why all the books. He explained that he had set out on a quest 40 years ago to **"Find out what it was all about,"** and he has consequently read all of the relevant books that he could find. So I asked "What is the answer?" He replied, "Well I still do not know what it is about," but he then said, **"But no one else does either."** So that's the first point, so much of what happens is unexplainable. The second point is that for anyone that does profess to have the knowledge of what it is all about, there are millions of other people that would not have the same views. As VOLTAIRE said
"Doubt is unpleasant, but Certainty is absurd."

SO WHAT?

The question is how can we use these unknowns to help us? We do not have to go very far for the first one which is our own brain. As I understand it, approximately 60% of our brain is operating at a subconscious level and we are consequently unaware of what it is doing. Yet once in a while it does something interesting which pops out and surprises us. So how we can use this awesome subconscious brain power to good effect.

THE SUBCONSCIOUS MIND — A STORY

I am in no way qualified to discuss at probably any level of detail the working of the subconscious mind, but I can relate a situation that happened to me in my early career. I had just been seconded from a large business to a small computer business that was in serious distress and my job as the General Manager was to save it. With the enthusiasm of youth and inexperience I tried and threw myself into the task. Working long hours every day, no sleep, worried constantly, given up my exercise program. I was clearly spiraling down to a burn out. So I had a little chat with myself and developed the following technique, which still works for me. At the end of the working day I sat down in an almost meditative state and went through all the issues of the day and the actions for tomorrow. I then wrote them down (important), put them in a folder and ceremoniously closed that folder and left for the day taking nothing home.

The next morning I would come in and ceremoniously open the folder have a look and quite often let out a loud expression of angst! (cleaned up). The surprising point was how many of the solutions popped out of my head more readily than I thought, and my sleep was dramatically improved. I like to think that this process had programmed my subconscious mind in such a way that it was left to just get on with solving these problems without interrupting my conscious activities. I had the confidence to let my brain to get on with a few things while I dealt with something else. Someone knowledgeable about these things may read this and say utter nonsense or yes that is what was happening. The point is that **IT WORKED FOR ME** and because it worked **I BELIEVED IT TO BE TRUE**. I had developed a belief system that had made me cope with a pretty stressful period in my life and get through it.

BELIEF IN A "PERSON" OR "PROJECT" IS THE FIRST STEP TOWARDS SUCCESS

LOOKING AFTER YOU

WHY IMPORTANT?

The most important person to look after is yourself, not said in a selfish way. The point is that the more able and capable that you are, then the more effective that you are to look after those that really matter to you. For clarity I appreciate that you may well put your loved ones before you, but on a day-to-day basis your loved ones will require you to be fit and well and functioning effectively.

THE BODY

You may be responsible in part for the livelihood and general well-being of many people. You have a responsibility and duty of care to stay fit if for no other reason, "The respect of your team." Not professional athlete level, of course. But a few basic things to do.

Watch your weight / blood pressure
Limit the intake of food / alcohol / caffeine
Take exercise
Have a regular medical / physical check up

THE MIND

Stay fresh and alert
Get sleep / Take time to relax
Go smell the daisies once in a while
Keep it trained and stimulated (an important tool)

THE KNOWLEDGE

Keep up to date
Refresher courses
Network
Read this book often

THE SPIRIT

Each to his own. But we all have a degree of spirituality

Religion / Meditation / Yoga

I have personal views on any of these areas, which I will keep to myself

If they work for YOU. Great, that's all that matters in my opinion

BIG SECRET

If you ask people to help and treat them with respect,
providing they have clear objectives and support
coupled with minimum interference,
they will usually produce a good result!

FINALLY

A PET THEORY

I think that the management of PEOPLE is so fundamentally important that anyone that has responsibility for say more than 100 people, should be licensed to do so. The licenses would only be obtained after considerable training and a whole bank of references from people they have previously be managed.

WHY

Badly managed PEOPLE are a huge burden on the economy. They impact productivity through disengagement and absence, they often get ill more, drink more and eat more. This places a huge burden on the infrastructure of society. Massive cost impact.

REALITY

Clearly an unrealistic and fanciful thought. But hopefully you get the point. And you never know. Some of the employment laws today would have been totally fanciful 20 years ago, especially in Europe. Always hope and optimism!

PLUS

Anyone attending the training must read this book?

So I get to make a lot of money.

SELF-INTEREST AND GREED

The good old dependable when dealing with PEOPLE.

APPENDICES

STORIES

CHECK LISTS

COMMON TERMS AND ABBREVIATIONS

STORIES

> ## Stories make a point very well for the following reasons:

They enable points to be made in a non-threatening way.

People learn predominantly through personal experience and a story often represents a situation close to actual experience that are we able to relate to.

It enables complex and varied points to be represented in an easy to relate way.

They can often be interesting and humorous. Therefore, easy to remember and repeat.

They can be repeated as an inspirational tool. Although the line between inspirational and boring can be close!

It enables the teller to show a more human and maybe fallible side of themselves. Good in small amounts.

People relate and usually have a story of their own. Bonding.

THE NEXT FEW PAGES INCLUDE SOME STORIES WITH THE RELATED SERIOUS POINTS. ALL TRUE AND PERSONAL.

STORIES

WHAT IS YOUR HORSE'S NAME?

On vacation in the Greek islands I decided to provide a little insight into how to get on with people to my three young children.

So, we approached a line of locals who were giving horse and cart rides.

I pick out the most miserable driver with the most decrepit horse.

This man just did not want to be doing this job.

So, we all pile into the carriage and with a grunt the driver starts.

After a short while I start the lesson. "So, what's your name?" I ask.

Signs of life and some communication. "And what's your horse's name?"

Animated response and the driver's whole attitude changed.

The lesson from dad was a raving success.

Unfortunately, for several years after that whenever the family all jumped into a cab and I asked the driver what his name was, it was followed quickly by a chorus of:

"And what's your horse's name?"

It can sometimes be a cross helping people to understand!

THE POINT

Classic Carnegie. How to win friends and influence people. Used favorite name and suspect favorite subject, him and his horse. Works nearly every time.

STORIES

DON'T FORGET THE FLOWERS

In a complex capital sale to a large UK utility, we were asked for a reference site for the customer to visit – naturally San Francisco was selected, as Manchester (UK) did not have the same appeal.
The trip cost our company £20,000 with airfares, entertainment, etc. Our Sales VP thoughtfully sent flowers to the customers' wives cost £100.
We got the order and guess what they remember most!

THE POINT

Small acts of thoughtfulness and kindness are very powerful. Plus do not forget that most of us have someone back at the ranch that we need to give some attention to and guess what, a few flowers may be a lot more important to them than a multi million dollar deal is to you because it shows that you CARE. (That word again!)

NEARLY WIPED OUT ON THE ROAD

Lovely sunny day driving along not a care in the world just switching lanes on the highway, quick look in the rear view mirror, did not signal moved over. Heard this great motor horn and looked in mirror, which was filled with a huge truck lights flashing a few feet from my rear. Hit the gas pedal, fortunately a fast car and got out of trouble.

THE POINT

I did not bother to signal because I thought the road was clear. I just did not know what I did not know! If I had done what was the correct control procedure it would have given someone else, in this case the truck driver, the opportunity of maybe stopping me pulling over or at least mitigate the outcome of my actions. One of the reasons we have controls and cross references, checks and balances is quite often "To find out what we do not know!" Plus, it provides other people with the opportunity to help and keep us out of trouble, maybe? So use them. Now a really interesting point, I hope? When people are in a metal box flying along detached from other people they often behave in a way that they would not even thing about in a closer interpersonal situation. They act aggressively, push people out the way, give abusive gestures. Imagine that your job role is the car, the office, the title etc. When you are in your "managerial car" make sure that you behave in a people related way. So many managers think that they have to some how behave differently because of the job. How we behave defines us. In or out a car, real or metaphoric.

STORIES

ONLY THE CHAIRMAN'S NIECE

Salesman arrives in reception for an appointment with a top customer and finds a new receptionist, who clearly is not up-to-speed on the company and procedures or the salesman (very new car outside). Eventually the salesman blows the receptionist out the water. He meets his customer, and during the polite opening chat finds out that his favorite niece was covering reception for a couple of weeks during her college vacation – oops!!
Bit like the people who treat secretaries and PAs with no courtesy... anyone messing with an assistant can often be in trouble big time...
they nearly always tell the boss afterwards!

THE POINT

The point is that in a collection of human beings, relationships may exist. Formal, family, interest groups, lovers, you never know all the intricate aspects of the interpersonal relationships in a large team.
Being a bit naughty, they can sometimes be used to advantage as you are able to use informal communication that hits the spot through diverse channels...
dangerous but can be fun!
I also believe you can tell a lot about a person by the way they treat people they "perceive" not to be important to them.

FIND THE OVERCOAT

Not one of mine, but from an authentic source. I do have many examples that make the same point. But I like this one.
A sales guy in California was asked by his company to visit New York in winter. This was a special trip not within the normal remit of this person. He had to buy a large overcoat just because of this trip so he put the cost of the coat on his next expense claim. His argument being that this was an entirely related business expense, as he did not require one for his personal lifestyle. The expense claim was thrown out. The aggrieved sales person re-submitted the claim with a stronger argument and again it was thrown out. So on the next expense claim submitted, which was pretty large and covered many items with no mention of the coat. He just put a little note for his boss, "Find the coat?"

THE POINT

People have away of getting what they want if they feel strongly about it. I was told this story about 8 years ago, must have repeated it several times and it makes a business point. The power of stories, they work long-term.

STORIES

THE FISH VAN

So, my first job as a CEO, and a small manufacturing unit has to be closed and moved to the main works. Approximately 30 long-serving people, mainly women assembly workers, average length of service 15 years.

Being keen and wanting to communicate the exercise well, I thought through all the issues and rehearsed my announcement.

Night before, a touch nervous and lost a little sleep, the day comes and I stand up and lay out the issues and actions, to be met with that sea of blank faces (as is often the case by the way and should not discourage you from mass communications).

"Any Questions?" I ask.

"Will the fresh fish van that comes on Tuesdays be allowed to call at the main works?"

"Will we be able to play Bingo on the main works announcement system during break time?"

THE POINT

People often have personal agenda items / issues that may not even be in the visibility of the leader.
Find out what is important to the team, it may help you achieve what is important to you.

STORIES

THE DAY THAT I CAUSED A SHOP FLOOR WALK OUT

The situation. I was 22, my first real experience with people. It was a section of 200 largely women assembly workers in a factory. A total learning experience by any standards!! This one young lady about my age was constantly late and we did have proper processes for disciplining poor attendance. But I thought no need for all that nonsense, I know her quite well. I thought a quiet word would be enough. I asked her to pop into my office, shut the door explained the situation. A really nice chat, said she understood and left. About 30 minutes later the works manager comes steaming into my office wanting to know why all my section had their coats on and were walking out. I of course had no idea what to do. So my boss gets this young lady's section into the office and asked what had gone on. She had apparently gone back to her bench and told them what I had said, but that she explained that she was always late because she had to work with a load of moaning old women, which I had agreed with. The girl in question burst into tears, the other woman realized what had happened and went back to work, the girl then said she would now have to leave. I then spent 15 minutes persuading her to stay.

THE POINT, SO MANY MISTAKES

I broke a cardinal rule, never discipline anyone without another person present.

I failed to understand that by taking her into my office (away from her territory) she then had to go back to her workplace with a plausible story.

I failed to understand that people behave differently when in a group v. when alone.

A quiet word in the ear, IF considered to be a good idea, should be discrete and on the other person's territory or a neutral place.

I failed to make any notes of the meeting, so it was her word against mine. Good job she did not bluff it out. Could have been a problem for me.

I confused a friendly buddy situation and forgot that I was the MANAGER.

THE REAL POINT
I knew everything I have just listed, but had to find out through experience.

STORIES

BAD PEOPLE

I was acting as an advisor for a small business in London that wanted to diversify its project range. We were invited to attend a pitch from an international company selling the rights for a muscle testing machine. Which was clearly rubbish technically, (without boring you about the technology of strain gauges on non-rigid surfaces) the lead presenter was interesting. He was immaculately dressed lots of gold everywhere and fake tan with the line visible just below his neck. I was a bit suspicious and they were selling quite aggressively and I honestly did not feel like saying no to them. My nose was twitching big time. So I constructed a load of conditions that I knew were unacceptable and they consequently threw us out. Good result. About a year later I was reading an article alleging that "organized crime" had been trying to access the London Venture Capital market with a fake muscle testing product. (Hope they are not reading this.) A couple of other related stories, I have been in a meeting in Italy with a very well respected large company and I asked one of the guys how he could be certain of something and he just opened his coat tapped a gun and smiled. A long time ago and I do not recall any other details. I have also been threatened with being thrown down a lift shaft for asking too many of the right questions. All very isolated incidents in a long career, but bad people do exist.

THE POINT

Not everyone that you meet is going to be well meaning honest and of high integrity. The prospect of making money will attract criminal activity. Be healthily cynical, if it looks too good to be true, it may well be. Plus, negotiations take on a different perspective when your personal safety may be an issue.

STORIES

KINDERGARTEN TEACHER

I was discussing this book with well respected colleague and he was telling me about a very effective GM. This GM had received no formal business training but was leading a team doing some great things. When asked for his secret he said that he had been a Kindergarten teacher and so much that he had learned applied to his current leadership role.

THE POINT

Human behavior can frequently be very basic. Sometimes management can get in the way of the simple and effective.

THE FROG AND THE SCORPION

Several years ago I attended a dinner organized by a large bank essentially as a thank you and marketing exercise for its customers. The layout included several tables of customers each with a bank exec as host. The closing speech was made by the head of banking for the region who unfortunately had little charisma and public speaking was definitely not his forte. One of his people must have told him to tell a story. He told the one about the frog and the scorpion. They were both trapped on an island with a rapidly approaching fire and the only way out was to get across a river. The frog could clearly swim, but the scorpion could not. The frog did not want to carry the scorpion across because they were enemies and the frog thought that when he crossed he would be stung and killed. After a debate the scorpion assured the frog that he would do no such thing for saving his life. The frog was convinced and they went across the river. When they got to other side, sure enough the scorpion stung and killed the frog. As the frog lay dying he looked at the scorpion and said, "Why?" To which the Scorpion replied, "I could not help it. It's in my nature." The bank executive then compared the bankers to the scorpion by saying that the way they behave is because it is in our nature as we are at heart all bankers.

THE POINT

Nearly every bank customer in the room thought something different. You bankers live off our backs and then when you are done with us leave us for dead. If you are not a natural storyteller, stick to boring, be safe. Who ever advised him, if anyone did, was crazy. Check that stories work. If in doubt, don't.

STORIES

THE DISAPPEARING ACT

I spent several happy years in the brewing industry, when it was largely run by brewers and way before health and safety laws and regulations had reached the workplace. Alcohol was present on a regular basis and the industry as you can imagine had many characters and a legion of stories. This is one of my favorites. The group chairman was visiting our brewery and the senior execs were all standing round in a large room in groups of three or four waiting for the chairman to do his rounds and come and meet everyone with the usual whimsical chat that people in high places and visiting royalty tend to do. This was in a very old hotel with large bay windows that had curtains (drapes) at the front of the bay with a large space behind. One of our group was a well-known character and by now he was well gone. When the group chairman arrived he was gently rocking back and forwards on his heels and had his back to these large curtains. Just as the chairman arrived this guy gently rocked back too far and fell though the curtains, which gently parted and then closed back after he had fallen through them, followed by the sound of a crumpled heap hitting the floor. Being British we all just carried on as if nothing had happened of course, and then rescued the guy (who fell asleep!) from behind the curtains after the chairman had gone.

THE POINT

It was very funny. But I suppose the real point is that alcohol and the workplace are dangerous bedfellows and should be used with care. FYI, my definition of the workplace is whenever and wherever you are in the presence of someone on the payroll or someone that has a business relationship with your business. Reputations and careers can be ruined in a night of madness.

STORIES

THE YOGA INSTRUCTOR

Sitting chatting to a very well qualified Yoga practitioner she was explaining that she had just been on an instructors' course. I asked what does that involve if you know all about Yoga. She explained. For example, most people would say "Raise and circle your left arm," where as the trained instructor would say, "Left arm raise and circle." Pretty obvious, really. In the first instruction the brain has to listen to 4 words before it realizes that it is about your left arm and an action is required. So this got me thinking about how we speak and write in business and so often these communications include many words before the subject is clear. Examples. The board met on Friday with everyone present at the meeting to discuss if they should approve the acquisition of a new car for the chairman. **Should maybe be:** The car for the chairman was approved .... Another example in the way we speak. I was with Mary the other day and we realized that we had not been out together for some time and there happens to be a concert on in the park next week, so I asked her if she would like to come. **Should maybe be:** There is a concert in the park next week, would you like to...... This only happened a few months ago and it has changed the way I write and speak. Amazing that it took so long.

THE POINT

Learning is an ongoing experience and some interesting stuff comes from the least expected place. If you are constantly talking to people to develop your "People Skills," surprising things can happen.

STORIES

WHAT WAS YOUR NAME AGAIN?

An early lesson about moving on and not looking back. I started as an apprentice on the shop floor age 17. This involved working in various departments for typically 2 or 3 months. My first department and new to the world of work was great and everyone treated me well, except for the odd joke they played on apprentices (like sending me to the wages department and asking for a form to opt out of the TAX club). The time came to move on, all said our good-byes, best apprentice ever, great working with you, etc. Off I went. A couple of weeks later I thought that I would pop back to see them. Initial greetings fine then after about 5 minutes I realized that life had moved on, another great apprentice in place and they had things to do so I reluctantly just left feeling in the way. Great that I learned that very early.

THE POINT

If you have to move on, try not to go back unless you really have made some good friends. Work buddies, however close, are work buddies, and work is the operative word. I think that this especially traumatic for very long-serving people about to retire or maybe have been laid off ahead of time. If they are not used to constant change then this can be very difficult to deal with. There is a Jack Nicholson film called "About Schmidt," which is a black comedy about this subject. I think it should be shown as a documentary for people about to retire and for managers to get them to maybe understand the emotions that these long-serving people are maybe going through.

THE QUESTION THAT THREW ME

I was recently talking to a group of graduates about the role of the CEO. One of them asked, "You must make so many decisions on a day-to-day basis, how do you cope with that?' I tried to think of the last time that I had made a major decision and it was difficult. Most of the time I support the decisions that the team brings for approval. Not so much me deciding as backing someone else's request / decision.

THE POINT

Top managers are looking for people who champion an idea and that the person feels passionate about. Then the decision is "if" to support that person more than the decision. Operating at the top levels in a business, it is mainly about trust and confidence in your team rather than making decisions for them.

STORIES

CHARMAINE

When I was writing this book I went to stay in a hotel for a few days, and visited the lounge where the hostess was a young lady called Charmaine. As usual, I asked how are you and where did you get that name from as it was not a local one. She said that her parents had named her after a song and that one day she would find out its history. So I just popped over to the computer hit the Internet, printed out a one-page history of the song and gave it to her. Her face really lit up, I mean really lit up, and I just said "Great, enjoy," and left. Guess what sort of service I had for the next few days. A few free drinks, genuinely treated really well, like a long lost friend. What a great investment for about 5 minutes of consideration. As I was writing this book I came back on the second day and watched how the various people treated Charmaine when they came in the lounge. Everyone had to make contact and sign in. The results really surprised me. I observed 40 people, all ages, sexes and probably 5 or so different countries. Most people were polite, respectful and said please and thank you in the right place. Just two I defined as just rude. This is the real surprising fact, not one person mentioned her name despite it being on a badge. Five people did make some nice pleasant conversation and showed an interest in her, which she appreciated. For the other 35 people she was just someone sitting behind a desk. I have absolutely no idea on the statistical relevance of this sample but if you include me, only 1 person in 41 mentioned her name. Depressing at so many levels.

THE POINT

For an investment of few minutes of time my experience in that hotel was better and cost me less money. This is the real good one. Every time I went in the lounge she would beam and smile and say, "How are you today Mr. Moore?" Most people in there would look up and maybe think, "Who is that guy, he must be important?" So payback in kind. How come then that 40 people did not make any effort to do the same? How come 40 people did not know that ONE WORD was the key to free drinks, superior service and being made to feel special. I was tempted not to put this little secret in the book, so I sneaked it in at the back. Would not like too much competition. I know you will not believe this, but just as I was finishing that sentence Charmaine came across the lounge beaming and said, "How are you tonight Mr. Moore?" I said, "Great. I am just writing about you in my book." She smiled and walked away not believing it for one minute. But that is a whole other point about why she did not believe me. It is in the way you tell it.

CHECK LISTS
A POWERFUL TOOL

Check lists can be used as aides to doing things like the following,

OR

You should also create your own action check lists

to monitor progress and activity.

I am such a huge fan of check lists that I actually put things on that I have already done to have the satisfaction of crossing them off!!

1. GETTING PEOPLE TO CHANGE
2. MOTIVATE THE TEAM
3. SUCCESSFULLY COMMUNICATE IDEAS
4. LEAD AND COMMAND RESPECT
5. STRESS RELIEF
6. NEGOTIATIONS
7. JOB OF A LEADER
16. HIRE GOOD PEOPLE
18. RUN A MEETING
19. DO A POWER POINT PRESENTATION
20. EMOTIONAL INTELLIGENCE
22. FATAL ERRORS THAT CAUSE BUSINESS FAILURE
24. SPEAKING
26. LOOK AFTER YOURSELF
27. MANAGE THE BOSS
32. NOT ALWAYS ABOUT MONEY
33. HOW TO GIVE PRAISE
34. HOW TO FIRE SOMEONE

♦1 GET PEOPLE TO CHANGE

Start with praise for the person concerned
Mention your own mistakes in area
Talk about the effects of old behavior
Explain the benefits of new behavior
Tell them capable of changing
Make the first part of change easy
Make sure the change means
    no loss of face
Agree targets for changed behavior
Monitor and encourage new behavior
Avoid words. Good and bad. Right or wrong
Perception is a form of reality

♦2 MOTIVATE THE TEAM

Be clear about own goals
Inform everyone of theirs
Give the right training
Coach and encourage
Listen to members
Get to know individuals
Incentivize everyone
Be tough when necessary
Give people space to grow
Let them get on with it

♦3 SUCCESSFULLY COMMUNICATE IDEAS

Tell it like it is
If you really believe it show it
Listen before you think and speak
Headlines first then whole story
Consistent clear message
If important, face-to-face
Involvement best persuader
Encourage feedback, act on it
Little and often better than long and loud
Communication works when
    things change

♦4 LEAD AND COMMAND RESPECT

Passionately believe in your vision
Build a team that shares your vision
Work harder than anyone else
Keep your problems to yourself
Tell team exactly what you expect
    from them
Listen to team. Respect their skills
Keep everyone informed
    and motivated
Give clear orders make sure happen
Share the profits
Very occasionally be ruthless

♦5 STRESS RELIEF

Learn to say no
Take exercise
Stay healthy
Meditation / yoga
Take time away to think
Stay professionally detached
Watch what you eat and drink
Avoid alcohol and caffeine
Change routines. Like route to work
Keep your sense of humor
Trust your subconscious
Socialize

♦ 6 NEGOTIATIONS
Do not fall in love with deal
Have a plan
Start early
Define objectives
Understand process
Define walk away position... Stick to it
Teamwork approach
Research other side
Do not get stranded
Build on consensus
Understand where power is
Make sure deal closed

♦ 7 JOB OF A LEADER
Agree strategy
Challenge thinking
Identify success criteria
Prepare plan / measure
Communicate
Select and manage team
Measure and monitor
Tidy up thinking
Recognize and reward
Reality check
Maintain discipline
Achieve objectives
Inspire and motivate
Follow and support
Develop people

♦ 16 HIRE GOOD PEOPLE
Get personally involved
Make the business attractive to work for
Ask good people to find good people
Involve the team
Do not rely on the HR process. Hijack it
Start with selling the company to them
Close offers quickly and personally

♦ 18 RUN A MEETING
Check right people attend; no more, no less
Start on time
Start by stating purpose of meeting
Nominate note / minute person
Agree agenda and time line
Venue and format to suit purpose
Quick stand up meetings very effective
Chair to keep process tight
Close down rambling unless a creative event
Finish by asking if everyone satisfied
Read out key actions agreed get agreement
Agree follow up / next meeting, if required

♦ 19
DO A POWER POINT PRESENTATION

Don't unless you really have to
No one listens
Best case is they remember you were good
And a maximum of
3 points to take away
If you must,
Keep it short
Do not read out the slides

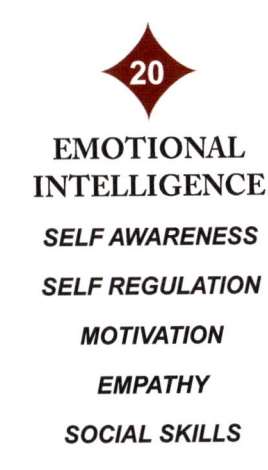

♦ 20
EMOTIONAL INTELLIGENCE

SELF AWARENESS

SELF REGULATION

MOTIVATION

EMPATHY

SOCIAL SKILLS

♦ 22
FATAL ERRORS THAT CAUSE BUSINESS FAILURE

Forget importance of profit
Not accept personal responsibility
Fail to develop people
Manage everyone the same way
Concentrate on problems not objectives
Not own personal development
Be a buddy not a boss
Fail to set standards
Recognize only top performers
Try to manipulate people
Try to control results not influence thinking

♦ 24
SPEAKING

Research the audience
Use three messages
Use body language
Voice is 38% of deal. Vary pitch on points
Dress to give good first impression
Connect with audience
Warm up before. Clear head
Know subject
Believe in yourself
Rehearse
Stress 3 points at end
Humour very powerful if works?

♦ 26
LOOK AFTER YOURSELF
Introduce stress reducing activities
Stay physically fit
Watch diet
Reduce alcohol, caffeine
Keep knowledge up-to-date
Read and network
Stay sociable and have outside interests
Take a break, clear the head

♦ 32
NOT ALWAYS ABOUT MONEY
Some Other Priorities

Safety of team members
Integrity of company
Quality and integrity of products
Personal issues of team members
Team morale
Team members welfare
Community support
Charity local and team members
Have fun reward performance

♦ 33
HOW TO GIVE PRAISE
Very Positive Motivator

Do as near event as possible
Not about you
Be personal mention name
Be sincere or not at all
Be specific about what done,
　　why good
Go public, let others know
Give something to remember
　　(e.g., letter, trophy)

♦ 27
MANAGE THE BOSS
Understand that you need to?
Work out their management style
The ultimate boss is the customer
Communicate properly and regularly
Identify bosses objectives / values
Focus on loyalty and support
Be assertive about longer-term issues
Communicate your agenda
Think how other people see you
Review actions and issues
Nip conflict in the bud
Talk to each other
Do not go over head. Unless?
Do not be aggressive
Deal with conflict in a controlled way

♦ 34
HOW TO FIRE SOMEONE
A Difficult and Often Emotional Area

Keep decision to let go business focused
Keep process to remove person focused
Make sure all processes are sound
Check all legal aspects with HR / lawyer
Become personally involved
Do not hide behind HR
Remember two important points:
　　The rest of your team will be watching
　　The person going may become
　　　important. Work for customer?
Therefore, as much as possible be:
　　supportive / positive / professional
　　friendly / helpful on transition
Take it seriously and personal
It will be a big deal for the person
Avoid becoming macho man

COMMON TERMS AND ABBREVIATIONS

ENERGY	**Human energy very important**	**EGO**	Get in the way of so much!
AGENDA	Everyone has one. Find it	**ENDORPHINS**	Brain cell high following exercise
APOLOGY	Quick if required. Very effective	**EXERCISE**	Important to stay fit
CHECK LIST	Items that require to be done	**GREED**	Anticipate it. A lot about!
CULTURE	Vital to success	**HR**	Human Relations
DOWNSIZING	Process to reduce company / costs structure	**HUMOR**	Very effective use carefully, especially internationally
DO IT NOW	Just get on with it	**INCENTIVE**	Payment to get things done. Make sure targeted effectively
DISCRIMINATION	Avoid at all times in all ways and in everything you do	**IQ**	Can be missing in high places
E MAILS	Eternal Record. Beware	**IF ONLY**	Move on. That was yesterday
		KISS	Keep It Simple Stupid (Sugar)
		LAW	Lots of it in the people area. Be careful
		LET GO	Sometimes you just have to

COMMON TERMS AND ABBREVIATIONS

MACHIAVELLIAN	Description of devious doing. Usually incorrect by some one that has not read "The Prince"	**TELEPATHY**	Does not really exist, but you probably rely on it!
OFFICE PARTY	Excellent opportunity to ruin your reputation	**TEMPUS FUGIT**	Time flees, or flies. It really does. Do something special make a contribution
MEETINGS	Keep them short, effective and focused	**THANK YOU**	Little used expression
MIND MAP / BRAIN PATH	Technique for creative thinking. Very effective	**TIME MANAGEMENT**	Does not exist. It's YOU Management
MOTIVATION		**TIME OUT**	Smell the daisies once in awhile
SERENDIPITY	Unexpected good outcome from an unrelated event	**TRAINING**	Essential to keep everyone up to speed and effective
SILENCE	Under-rated negotiating tool	**TRUST**	Very important and it starts at the TOP
SLEEP	Important. Get some	**WEIGHT**	Watch it. You will feel better for it
SOPORIFIC	My favorite word. Just never get to use It	**VACATION**	Take one
SUCCESSION PLANNING	The route to your next promotion	**WHY**	Ask it often!
STORIES	Excellent way to communicate	**WORK**	Something you are PAID to do. Keep the PAID to DO bit in mind!
S W O T	Excellent way to waste the time of a lot of people	**YIELD**	Return on assets or equities
TALK	If you have to. Listening is far more effective		
TEAM	A group of people with a common objective. The collective output ideally being higher than the sum of the individual parts		
YOU	Most important asset, look after it!	**R I P**	Run out of CASH

Made in the USA
Charleston, SC
02 June 2013